STYLE AND SOCIETY
IN GERMAN
LITERARY EXPRESSIONISM

by Egbert Krispyn

University of Florida Monographs

HUMANITIES

No. 15, Winter 1964

STYLE AND SOCIETY
IN GERMAN
LITERARY EXPRESSIONISM

by Egbert Krispyn

University of Florida Monographs
HUMANITIES
No. 15, Winter 1964

UNIVERSITY OF FLORIDA PRESS / GAINESVILLE, FLORIDA

PREFACE

Even a modest monograph cannot be written without incurring many debts of gratitude to people and institutions. I should like to acknowledge specifically those to Dr. Adolf D. Klarmann to whom, among numerous other things, I owe many insights into literature generally and expressionism particularly; to Dr. Melvin E. Valk for untiring assistance and support; and to the Alexander von Humboldt-Stiftung which some years ago enabled me to spend much time in Germany, mainly on the study of expressionism. This monograph is partly based on some ideas which I first presented in the context of my doctoral dissertation "Georg Heym and the Early Expressionist Era," written for the University of Pennsylvania under the supervision of Professor Klarmann. And my thanks must of course go to the Graduate School of the University of Florida for making possible this publication.

March, 1964   EGBERT KRISPYN

CONTENTS

Introduction   1

The Price of Glory   8

In Zarathustra's Footsteps   16

Expressionists and Expressionism   25

The Pattern of Pathos   44

The Definition at Work   53

Book List   60

INTRODUCTION

In Germany the word "expressionism" gained currency as a literary term between 1912 and 1914. Exactly who first used it in connection with literature, and when and where, cannot be established with certainty. The word was coined around the turn of the century in France, with reference to the pictorial arts. In 1911 the German art historian Wilhelm Worringer employed the term in the framework of his aesthetic theory which, to counter the then current naturalistic-materialistic emphasis on technical know-how, postulated the primacy of the artist's will and intention.[1]

The association in Worringer's theories of the term "expressionism" with the concept of art as a volitive manifestation set a trend also in the word's subsequent literary usage. In discussions of literary expressionism the outlook and personality of the writer frequently are more important than the works. Thus Ferdinand Josef Schneider asks, with typical emphasis on the author's intention, "Was will nun eigentlich der Expressionismus oder die Ausdruckskunst?" And he arrives at the following conclusion: "Die Ausdruckskunst will, dass der Einzelne seine trostlose Isolierung innerhalb des Weltalls aus tiefster Seele empfinde und daher in brennendster Sehnsucht nach der Vereinigung mit allen Teilen des Universums ringe, mit andern Worten, dass jeder Einzelne sich kosmisch ausweite."[2]

For contemporary and near-contemporary commentators who were themselves, in the phrase coined by Albert Soergel, "im Banne des Expressionismus" and wrote from a position of immediacy and involvement, this concentration on the human element is natural and legitimate. It does not, however, provide an adequate foundation for objective inquiry into the expressionist movement. The literary-historical perspective also demands purely literary criteria. Attempts were made quite early to find these in the expressionists' use of language.

1. See, among others, Albert Soergel and Curt Hohoff, *Dichtung und Dichter der Zeit. Vom Naturalismus bis zur Gegenwart* (Düsseldorf, 1963), II, 27-28, 324; Gottfried Benn, Introduction to *Lyrik des expressionistischen Jahrzehnts. Von den Wegbereitern bis zum Dada* (Wiesbaden, 1955), pp. 6 ff; Kasimir Edschmid, Preamble to *Frühe Manifeste. Epochen des Expressionismus*, in "die mainzer reihe" (Hamburg, 1957), I, 9 ff; Wilhelm Duwe, *Deutsche Dichtung des 20. Jahrhunderts vom Naturalismus zum Surrealismus* (Zürich, 1962), pp. 21-22.
2. *Der expressive Mensch und die deutsche Lyrik der Gegenwart* (Stuttgart, 1927), p. 7.

1

Kasimir Edschmid is typical of the dominant tendency towards a personality-centered approach when in 1917 he declares of expressionism, "Sie ist kein Programm des Stils. Sie ist eine Frage der Seele."[3] Nevertheless, among the seven-thousand-odd words of the essay concerned, Edschmid includes the following characterization of what he calls expressionist language:

Auch das Wort erhält andere Gewalt. Das beschreibende, das umschürfende hört auf. Dafür ist kein Platz mehr. Es wird Pfeil. Trifft in das Innere des Gegenstands und wird von ihm beseelt. Es wird kristallisch das eigentliche Bild des Dinges.

Dann fallen die Füllwörter.

Das Verbum dehnt sich und verschärft sich, angespannt so deutlich und eigentlich den Ausdruck zu fassen.

Das Adjektiv bekommt Verschmelzung mit dem Träger des Wortgedankens. Auch es darf nicht umschreiben. *Es* allein muss das Wesen am knappsten geben und nur das Wesen.

Sonst nichts.[4]

Whatever concrete observations are contained in this statement obviously are not valid for all authors who are traditionally regarded as expressionists. There is nothing particularly arrow-like about the words in the following passage from a story by Georg Heym, which contains expletives galore, while the use of verbs is quite unremarkable and the adjectives are plainly descriptive:

So sah er einmal vor einem weinroten Grunde den Teufel über einem Haufen von schwarzen Leibern, die ihn anbeteten; ein andermal sah er eine ungeheure Fledermaus, die mit ausgespannten Flügeln an den Himmel angeschlagen zu sein schien, wie sie von den Bauern an die Türen der Scheunen genagelt wird, oder einen riesigen Dreimaster, oder Bäume auf Bergen, oder gewaltige Löwen, ungeheuere Schlangen, die um die Schultern des Himmels gelegt waren, oder einen riesigen Mönch in einer schleppenden Soutane, oder Männer mit seltsamen langen Profilen, und einmal einen feurigen Engel, der mit einer grossen Fackel über die Treppen des Äthers stieg.[5]

Yet Georg Heym, who died in January, 1912, before the word "expressionism" had gained vogue, was in retrospect recognized to be one of the most prominent exponents of this movement. This only confirms that the

3. *Frühe Manifeste,* p. 40.
4. *Ibid.,* p. 38.
5. Heym, "Der Dieb," in *Dichtungen und Schriften. Gesamtausgabe,* Vol. II: *Prosa und Dramen,* ed. Karl Ludwig Schneider (Hamburg, München, 1962), p. 73.

2

type of language which Edschmid describes and manifests in his own style is by no means characteristic of expressionist writing generally. Recognizing this fact, later commentators such as R. H. Thomas and Richard Samuel have attempted to supplement Edschmid's description in order to do justice to the various "aspects of Expressionist style and language in so far as these kept within the bounds of comprehensibility."[6] Thus they declare, "While the device of word-accumulation reflects the breathlessness, exaltation and ecstasy of Expressionist style, the application of parallelisms and antitheses corresponds more to the rational tendencies which we noted in Expressionism side by side with the emotional elements."[7]

The observation that within the body of literature commonly classified as expressionist the language was handled in contradictory and mutually exclusive ways indicates the impossibility of finding a literary criterion of expressionism in this direction. Faced with the dilemma that an analysis of the texts does not yield any distinguishing literary-linguistic characteristics common to them all, several reactions are possible. One can conclude that there are absolutely no unifying elements, and therewith in effect discard the term "expressionism" and refute the judgment of those who originally applied it to designate a specific type of writing. Wilhelm Emrich exemplifies this viewpoint. "Völlig Unvereinbares geht in die literarische Revolution von 1910-1925 ein und scheint ihr das Bild eines undurchschaubaren Wirbels widerstreitender Kräfte zu verleihen."[8]

One may evade the difficulty by using an impenetrable pseudo-profound jargon—a procedure which Walter Muschg has analyzed in his remarks on "zerschwatzte Dichtung."[9] Gottfried Benn points out that many of the mutually contradictory interpretations of expressionism that he quotes are couched in an obscure prose which in itself characterizes their contents. But Benn himself lapses into the same type of tortuous language for which he criticizes his predecessors, as soon as he postulates his own definition of the expressionist style. "Dieser Stil . . . vielfältig in seiner empirischen Abwandlung, einheitlich in seiner inneren Grundhaltung als Wirklichkeitszertrümmerung, als rücksichtloses An-die-Wurzel-der-Dinge-Gehen bis dorthin, wo sie nicht mehr individuell und sensualistisch gefärbt, gefälscht, verweichlicht verwertbar in den

---

6. *Expressionism in German Life, Literature and the Theatre (1900-1924)* (Cambridge, 1939), p. 157.
7. *Ibid.,* pp. 153-54.
8. *Protest und Verheissung. Studien zur klassischen und modernen Dichtung* (Frankfurt/M, Bonn, 1960), p. 148.
9. See *Die Zerstörung der deutschen Literatur* (Bern, München, 1958).

psychologischen Prozess verschoben werden können, sondern im akausalen Dauerschweigen des absoluten Ich der seltenen Berufung durch den schöpferischen Geist entgegensehen."[10]

More sympathetic, but no more productive, than this kind of verbiage is the attitude taken up by Curt Hohoff, who denies the possibility of defining the term, which he nevertheless uses freely. "Den Expressionismus jedoch gesetzmässig erfassen zu wollen, wäre ebenso vergeblich wie im Fall der berühmten Epochenbegriffe Barock und Romantik: es waren komplexe Bewegungen mit literarischen und ausserliterarischen Antrieben."[11]

Although this view is in line with the fashionable skepticism concerning "-isms," it is untenable. The present study intends to demonstrate that it is quite possible to define expressionism; moreover, the comparisons with baroque and romanticism are not to the point. Owing to the greater temporal distance and the smaller numbers of writers involved, the notions of German baroque and romanticism are for most practical purposes adequately circumscribed. The exponents and the borderline figures of these respective movements have on the whole been recognized and assigned to them, whereas the area of general agreement as to who is an expressionist includes only a fraction of those who have at one time or another been so called.

Moreover, the short duration of the expressionist movement meant that for a number of authors it represented only a passing phase in their development, so that within the works of, for instance, Georg Kaiser or Franz Werfel the lack of a definition is keenly felt. Most urgent, however, is the need for a clear concept of expressionism in determining the extent of its influence on post-World-War-II literature. If the dividing line between superficial similarities and profound interactions cannot be drawn, this has a detrimental effect on the understanding and appreciation of current writing. The need for a criterion of expressionism is thus predominantly practical, because without it the reader and the literary scholar lack an essential tool for the categorization and intellectual apprehension of a considerable part of twentieth century German literature.

Acknowledging, at least implicitly, the impossibility of deducing the essence of literary expressionism through analysis of its often apparently irreconcilable stylistic manifestations, recent scholarship tends to approach the problem from a sociological viewpoint. This amounts to a

10. *Lyrik des expressionistischen Jahrzehnts,* p. 11.
11. Soergel and Hohoff, p. 20.

4

continuation of the traditional stress on the author rather than the work, with the important distinction, however, that such rather vague and intangible factors as individual attitude and world view are traced back to their origin in concrete sociological facts. The most notable example of this approach is Walter Sokel's study, *The Writer in Extremis*, the title of which is symptomatic.[12] Although he makes many valuable observations on specific works, Sokel is primarily concerned with the human and social situation of the expressionists.

The results of this type of study have been most illuminating and, by isolating the sociological factors underlying the emergence of expressionism, have demonstrated the movement's unity at least on the level of its exponents' existential background. With specific reference to the literary manifestations, however, the sociologically oriented method of inquiry has so far not arrived at a satisfactory workable definition and has not yielded an adequate criterion of expressionism. It might be said that we know an expressionist is a "writer in extremis"—in the not quite literal meaning Walter Sokel attaches to this term—but what literary expressionism is, remains as obscure as before.

The lament with which Richard Brinkmann introduces his research report for the years 1952-1960 still holds good.

Den Namen "Expressionismus" für jene Literatur etwa des Jahrzehnts zwischen 1910 und 1920, des "expressionistischen Jahrzehnts," gebrauchen viele mit schlechtem Gewissen, weil sie nicht recht wissen, was er genau besagen soll. Und mit der Klage, dass gar nicht feststehe, was Expressionismus eigentlich sei, hebt manche Darstellung an, in der irgend etwas über Expressionismus steht. Erstaunlich oft, ja meist, liest man in monographischen Abhandlungen über einen expressionistischen Dichter an der Stelle, wo das spezifisch Expressionistische seines Werkes geklärt werden soll, "eigentlich expressionistisch," wie das der "eigentlichen Expressionisten," sei es gar nicht. Wer diese "eigentlichen Expressionisten" aber sind, wo das Mass für das Expressionistische zu suchen sei, das wird selten gesagt und fast nie genau.[13]

12. Walter H. Sokel, *The Writer in Extremis. Expressionism in 20th Century German Literature* (Stanford, Calif., 1959). The fact that the title of the German edition—*Der literarische Expressionismus* (München, n.d.)—thus does not fit the contents and creates a false impression of the author's aim is largely responsible for the critical reception it had. See H. Kasack, "Deutsche Literatur im Zeichen des Expressionismus," *Merkur*, XV (1960). For a penetrating survey of the literature on expressionism, see Kurt Mautz, *Mythologie und Gesellschaft im Expressionismus. Die Dichtung Georg Heyms* (Frankfurt/M, Bonn, 1961), Chapter I.
13. *Expressionismus. Forschungs-Probleme 1952-1960* (Stuttgart, 1961), pp. 1-2.

The attempt in the following pages to find a yardstick for expressionism does not pretend to refute the fruits of previous studies on the subject. The aim is, rather, to interpret and combine facts, which for the greater part are not new, in such a manner that they point the way out of the present impasse concerning the definition of expressionism.

Past attempts have proved the futility of trying to arrive at a common literary denominator for the works generally regarded as expressionist through an analysis of their linguistic peculiarities. The conclusion that one cannot speak of a typical expressionist style in that sense appears to be inescapable. A comprehensive concept of style does, however, go beyond the details of usage and refers to a general creative attitude.[14] This is not the author's private outlook on the world, but the consistent structural pattern of his writings in which his opinions creatively manifest themselves. If a common style in this meaning of the word can be established, which fits those works which are practically unanimously and wholeheartedly called expressionist, it could be used as a criterion in dealing with borderline cases, forerunners, and successors.

To arrive at such a stylistic yardstick one could possibly follow various methods. The one applied in the following pages uses the sociological approach to expressionism as its starting point. The reasons are twofold. First, by tracing the genesis of the common expressionist style from the common sociological background of the expressionists, the danger of "Hineininterpretieren" is diminished. Second, the sociological aspects of expressionism have been so well investigated that they provide the soundest base for the exploration of the general stylistic mold of expressionist writing.

To overcome the methodological limitations which hitherto have prevented the exponents of the sociological approach from reaching any satisfactory conclusions about expressionist style, the gap between the personal sphere of experiences and opinions and the literary sphere of structural patterns has to be bridged. For this purpose textual interpretation has to be used. The stylistic traces of the ascertainable common expressionist attitude are followed in a number of very different works, and are revealed to be logical variants of one and the same basic pattern. In this context the sociological starting point proves its merit, because it provides the knowledge that works which are at first sight totally dissimilar, yet embody different realizations of one basic outlook on the

---

14. See Wolfgang Kayser, *Das sprachliche Kunstwerk* (Bern, 1948), p. 291: "Stil ist . . . von innen her gesehen die Einheit und Individualität der Perzeption, das heisst eine bestimmte Haltung."

6

world. The verifiable sociological data serve to guide the difficult exploration of the parallel configuration of phenomena on the stylistic level. Without insight into the various forms in which a common fundamental attitude can be realized in specific individual world views, it would be almost impossible to reconstruct the common denominator of the widely divergent literary patterns in the expressionists' works.

On the basis of these considerations, this study begins with a survey of the consequences which the socio-economical situation in Wilhelmian Germany had for the generations which the expressionists represent. Then it is shown how these circumstances affected and colored their attitude and world view. Most of the material in these first two chapters is familiar from previous sociological studies; the presentation, however, naturally stresses those aspects which are particularly relevant for the subsequent development of the inquiry. The third chapter incorporates the attempt to transcend the limitations of the sociological approach and executes the transition of the train of argument from the personal to the literary realm. The concept of expressionism which is thus developed is then interpreted in terms of traditional poetics and, finally, tested by application to a number of specific cases.

Something must here be said about certain aspects of the terminology employed in the following pages. The word "pathos" is used throughout in the frame of reference provided by German poetic theory, which precludes the often somewhat derogatory connotations the word has in normal American usage. It is here employed in the context of the human suffering caused by the discrepancy between reality and ideal, and hence, by derivation, related to this discrepancy itself. The word as used in this study should therefore not be associated with the customary American interpretation linking it with pity, sympathy, and tender sorrow.

The present use of the word "expressionism" also requires some preliminary comment. Until a definition of this term is arrived at—in the third chapter—this study for practical reasons uses the word in a general chronological sense, and to refer to writers and works commonly considered as representing the movement, as indicated by authoritative literary historical studies and anthologies.

1. THE PRICE OF GLORY

The expressionist movement, which is usually deemed to have lasted from 1910 till 1920—the "expressionist decade"—comprised with but few exceptions authors belonging to the generation born between 1885 and 1895.[1] They grew up in the pre-war Wilhelmian empire, which therefore provides the social frame of reference for their personalities. This is true also of those members of the expressionist generation, including such prominent figures as Werfel, Trakl, and Kafka, who were born and sometimes lived beyond the political borders of the German empire. The sociological conditions in Austria-Hungary at this time closely resembled those in Germany; moreover, the German-speaking bourgeoisie emulated to the best of its ability the style of life prevalent among its counterpart in the Reich.

The importance of the Wilhelmian era as the background of expressionism is further underlined by the fact that the movement's distinctive features were established during its initial phase from 1910 till 1914. The development during the war and post-war years, which radically changed the Wilhelmian pattern of life, led to a qualitative deterioration and an increasing admixture of unliterary, propagandistic elements which reflect the loss of the original social substratum on which the expressionist movement was founded.

This world which gave rise to expressionism was itself the product of the very intensive industrialization which in the decades following the Franco-Prussian War of 1870-1871 transformed the country's economic, social, and political structure.[2] The political unification of the empire, the feelings of national pride and optimism, and, above all, the huge French reparation payments helped Germany to overtake in a very brief time the established industrial states of Europe in the race towards the modern Machine Age. The rapid and thorough industrialization of the country was a national achievement of the first magnitude. It placed Germany on an equal industrial footing with England, which for more than a century had been the leading manufacturing nation of Europe.

1. See the biographies in *Menschheitsdämmerung. Ein Dokument des Expressionismus,* newly revised edition, ed. Kurt Pinthus (Hamburg, 1959).
2. The remarks on the historical and political aspects of the Wilhelmian empire are mainly based on Conrad Bornhak, *Deutsche Geschichte unter Kaiser Wilhelm II* (Leipzig, Erlangen, 1922); Martin Göhring, *Bismarcks Erben 1890-1945* (Wiesbaden, 1958); Theobald Ziegler, *Die geistigen und sozialen Strömungen Deutschlands im 19. und 20. Jahrhundert* (Berlin, 1916).

The suddenness and speed of this industrial revolution did, however, give rise to very serious social problems. The eruptive development of a factory proletariat, caused by the transformation of an agrarian country into a modern industrial state, made it inevitable that housing facilities and protective legislation should lag behind. The result was that the vast majority of the laborers lived under appalling conditions. The accomodations available to them were usually unhygienic and cramped, and therefore damaging to their physical and mental health. Wages were extremely low, working days of fourteen to sixteen hours were the rule, and there was no limitation on the employment of women and children from the age of four onwards.

Inevitably, this state of affairs led to great discontent among those concerned. An economic crisis in 1873, causing unemployment and in many cases a reduction of the already very low wages, was, through its widespread tragic consequences for the proletariat, instrumental in awakening their political consciousness. As this development constituted an obvious threat to the Establishment, two attempts on the Emperor's life were exploited to stir up public feeling against the socialists. As a result the Reichstag was prepared to pass the repressive Sozialistengesetz, which produced a lasting estrangement between the socialists on the one hand and the rest of the nation on the other.

A contributing factor in this development was the spread of militarism and nationalism from the upper classes down through the bourgeoisie. Officers from middle-class stock, who had participated in the campaign of 1870 in which the army had covered itself with glory, propagated these notions after the return to civilian occupations. Later the government, by stirring up anti-English feelings and promoting the idea of naval expansion, especially through the Flottenvereine, confirmed the bourgeoisie in its militaristic and nationalistic tendencies. In so doing, it widened the rift between the middle class and the proletariat which under the pressure of circumstances had become increasingly international in outlook.

The bourgeoisie, through lack of contact with the lower social strata with their social and political extremism, was deprived of a stimulus which conceivably could have prevented the rapid ossification of its views and concepts. The emergence of false and self-delusory, but sacrosanct, pseudo-idealistic values as a façade for its crass materialism was certainly hastened by the ideological isolation of the lower urban classes.

The changes in the structure of German society between 1871 and

9

1914, which gave rise to the emergence of an industrial proletariat, also affected the upper classes of landowners and higher officials. They lost their dominant position in the community to the industrial entrepreneurs, and the massive migration of agrarian laborers to the cities often left the landed aristocracy, especially in the eastern provinces, short of the workers needed to run their estates.

In addition, the rapid development in intensity and extent of international trade provided serious competition for primary producers. These circles naturally exerted their political influence to try to obtain the sort of protective legislation which was opposed to the interests of the industrial and commercial circles. Since the government needed the landowners' support, especially in the matter of military and naval expansion, this political agitation had considerable success. The extremely partisan attitude which the agrarian groups revealed in this connection did, however, seriously weaken their political prestige. Soon it became obvious that the landed aristocracy and the circles connected with it had irrevocably lost their struggle against the spirit of the age. Thus for this section of society the last decades before World War I were definitely a period of decay, in which all traditional values and ideas were irredeemably crumbling away. As a class, these people belonged to the past. Only in the past did they see virtue; the present and future held no appeal or promise for them.

With the old ruling class clinging to the past, and the proletariat fighting for the future, the present belonged to the bourgeoisie, which through its control over manufacture and trade determined the face of the new Germany. Even the figure of the Emperor appears from this viewpoint as a projection of the middle-class ideal of manly and patriotic virtues. The middle class put its stamp so decisively on every aspect of life in the empire that it might well have adopted Louis XIV's apocryphal motto: "L'état, c'est moi!"

But although the bourgeoisie in a material and political sense profited greatly from the industrial revolution, the sudden change in its established mode of living was, on the whole, far from beneficial. Upon this class, from which the expressionists almost to a man were recruited, the main sociological effect of the industrialization and urbanization was the final dissolution of the patriarchal pattern of existence.[3] The vast majority of the middle class became big-city dwellers.

Apart from the newly emerging factory proletariat, the bourgeoisie

3. For the social background of the expressionists, see the biographies in *Menschheitsdämmerung*.

10

was mainly responsible for the growth in number and size of the urban communities. Whereas at the end of the Franco-Prussian War the empire numbered only eight cities of more than 100,000 inhabitants, at the turn of the century this number had increased to thirty-three. Berlin in this period increased its population from 500,000 to almost 2,000,000,[4] and a similar, if less extreme, expansion took place in most other cities where industries were established.

In these large modern cities the traditional concept of the family as a large clan, headed and ruled by a patriarchal figure, could not survive. Its place was taken by the small unit of the individual household, in which the sense of continuity and tradition marking the large clan was lost. In this process the importance and authority pertaining to the position of the family father were severely curtailed. The patriarchal head of the clan had represented the idea of the family and derived his authority from it; the function of the household head was now reduced to providing for a temporally delimited group of individuals which formed part of a contemporary social stratum rather than of a continuous family history.

In the glow of pride and enthusiasm which the new achievements and prosperity engendered, however, this reduction in status was not acknowledged by the heads of the families. On the contrary, their feeling of having reached the ultimate stage in the development of humanity and their self-assertive tendencies, if anything, increased. Being no longer able to apply such urges to the clan as a whole, the Wilhelmian family father concentrated his authoritarian tendencies on his immediate domestic environment. As Hans Heinrich Muchow puts it, "Er versuchte nun diese Beeinträchtigungen mit Herrschsucht im Kreise seiner Familie zu kompensieren."[5]

By the time the expressionist generation was in its formative years, the discrepancy between the fathers' pretended authority and their actual position had become so glaring as to provoke the youngsters to rebellion. Moreover, the initial spirit of enterprise which had marked Germany's rapid progress to a position of industrial prominence had irrevocably deteriorated into an atmosphere of pedestrian materialism.

In this respect, too, the older generation refused to accept reality. They assumed a pseudo-idealistic stance which those adolescents who had be-

---

4. See Georg Reicke, "Die Groszstadt," *Die Neue Rundschau* (February, 1912), pp. 202-3.
5. Hans Heinrich Muchow, *Sexualreife und Sozialstruktur der Jugend* (Hamburg, 1959), p. 54.

come skeptical of their parents' authority soon recognized as spurious. The most uncompromising ones among the adolescents herewith in effect ostracized themselves from the Wilhelmian bourgeois society, which was based on acceptance of the idealized self-image of the average Wilhelmian bourgeois. The fathers, endeavoring to make their sons conform by the sheer weight of their suspect authority, only succeeded in widening the gap between themselves and the younger generation.

The fathers' attempt to force the younger generation to accept their dishonest world view had disastrous consequences for the adolescents' attitude towards them. An inter-generation conflict arose which manifested its social and environmental origin in the fact that it affected even those families where there seemed to be no immediate personal reason for its existence. In such cases the sons became the prey of ambivalent feelings. On the one hand they loved and respected the fathers, while on the other hand they felt themselves reluctantly caught up in the universal wave of hostility.

This feeling of being driven apart by forces beyond their control is clearly expressed by Franz Kafka when, in his *Brief an den Vater*, he remarks, "Ich glaube, Du seist gänzlich schuldlos an unserer Entfremdung. Aber ebenso gänzlich schuldlos bin auch ich."[6] Similarly Franz Werfel in the story *Nicht der Mörder, der Ermordete ist schuldig* sees the father-son conflict as an inescapable, supra-personal fate, when he lets the son ask his father the rhetorical question: "Oder stehen wir beide vor einem unbegreiflichen Gesetz, uns in der *Ferne suchen* und in der *Nähe hassen* zu müssen."[7] As these utterances indicate, the positive personal feelings, if any, were powerless against the atmosphere of the times, so that the relationship between father and son in almost all cases is characterized by a predominance of unusually intensive mutual hatred.

This central experience in the youth of the expressionist generation manifested itself in many of their works. Apart from the Werfel story, one could mention in this context Arnold Bronnen's *Vatermord*, Walter Hasenclever's *Der Sohn*, Reinhard Sorge's *Der Jüngling*, J. von der Goltz's *Vater und Sohn*, Alfred Wolfenstein's poem *Knabennacht*, Karl Otten's *Die Heimkehr*, Fritz von Unruh's *Ein Geschlecht* and Franz Kafka's *Das Urteil*. The evidence of these works and of the available biographical material confirms the statement made by Karl Otten in his survey of the expressionist era: "Fast allen Dichtern der hier zur Debatte stehenden Zeit widerfuhr das Schicksal des Vaterhasses, des Zerfalls

6. In *Die Neue Rundschau*, Vol. LXIII, No. 2.
7. München, Leipzig, 1920, p. 137.

12

mit der bürgerlichen Familie, dem besonders Walter Hasenclever, Franz Kafka, Georg Trakl und Franz Werfel dämonischen Ausdruck verliehen."[8]

As a consequence of this inescapable tendency towards severe intergeneration friction, the adolescents inflated the father's image to the point where it stood for every form of authority with which the rebellious youth was in a potential state of conflict. Franz Werfel expressed the significance of this hypertrophied father-figure. "Was versteht ihr unter —Herrschaft des Vaters?—Alles. Die Religion: denn Gott ist der Vater der Menschen. Der Staat: denn König oder Präsident ist der Vater der Bürger. Das Gericht: denn Richter und Aufseher sind die Väter von Jenen, welche die menschliche Gesellschaft Verbrecher zu nennen beliebt. Die Armee: denn der Offizier ist der Vater der Soldaten. Die Industrie: denn der Unternehmer ist der Vater der Arbeiter!"[9]

In this rhetorical outburst, Werfel fails to mention one aspect of repressive authority which in the life of the expressionist generation as well as in contemporary literature played a very major role. This was the school, which could be regarded as the most important extension of parental power. Frank Wedekind's *Frühlings Erwachen*, Max Halbe's *Jugend*, Lou Andreas-Salomé's *Ruth* and *Im Zwischenland*, Emil Strauss' *Freund Hein*, Hermann Hesse's *Unterm Rad*, Heinrich Mann's *Professor Unrat*, and Robert Musil's *Die Verwirrungen des Zöglings Törless* all deal with the fate of the artistically gifted or very sensitive youth at the Wilhelmian institution of secondary education.

For an evaluation of the predominantly negative role the schools played in the development of the generation we are not, however, dependent only on the sometimes subjective and biased evidence of works of fiction. There are also autobiographical notes on the subject, for instance by Stefan Zweig who with reference to the very similar Austrian educational system remarked, "Wir sollten vor allem erzogen werden, überall das Bestehende als das Vollkommene zu respektieren, die Meinung des Lehrers als unfehlbar, das Wort des Vaters als unwidersprechlich, die Einrichtungen des Staates als die absolut und in alle Ewigkeit gültigen."[10]

In their pursuance of the primary aim of preserving the status quo, the schools—and especially the Gymnasiums to which most of the bour-

---

8. Karl Otten, *Ahnung und Aufbruch. Expressionistische Prosa* (Darmstadt, 1957), p. 12.
9. *Nicht der Mörder, der Ermordete ist schuldig*, p. 99.
10. *Die Welt von Gestern* (Frankfurt/M, 1949), p. 50.

geois youngsters went—tenaciously clung to their hallowed humanist traditions which, however, had long since become fossilized and as decrepit as the system they were to defend.

The educators' attitude towards the predominantly philological subject matter is revealed in an autobiographical note by Rudolf G. Binding. "Man schulte den Verstand, man übte das Gehirn, man trainierte auf sprachliche uneigene Form durch das beständige Fussexerzieren in der lateinischen Sprache, in der Mathematik, in der Grammatik und Syntax, in dem fremden Formenreich der griechischen. Dazu wurden die alten Sprachen missbraucht. Von ihrem Geist habe ich keinen Hauch verspürt."[11] A similar negative judgment on the state of teaching at the Gymnasiums was expressed by the highly regarded contemporary pedagogue Ludwig Gurlitt, when he referred to their "bureaukratisch nüchterne, philologisch pedantische und nur den Buchstaben dienende Tätigkeit."[12]

However, dissatisfaction with the schools was not limited to the pupils and a few perceptive insiders. Among the population generally, as well as in official quarters, there was strong criticism of the educational system. The perspective in these circles was, to be sure, very different from that of the pupils, who felt that they were the victims of a repressive and reactionary system intended to force them to submit to the spurious views and values of their fathers. From the viewpoint of the average middle-class citizen the schools were too intellectualized, and did not do justice to the emotional, nationalistic idealism on which he prided himself. Hence the unprecedented success of a book like Julius Langbehn's *Rembrandt als Erzieher,* which in a few years after its original, anonymous publication in 1889 went through more than forty editions. Langbehn represented the chauvinistic mysticism and hysterical anti-intellectualism into which the bourgeoisie escaped from the materialistic reality of their petty everyday life. Understandably, *Rembrandt als Erzieher* was completely devoid of any constructive ideas.

A more honest approach prevailed among educational officials, but their criticism of the secondary schools was also of an entirely different nature from that of the pupils. From the official viewpoint the inadequacy of the system was bound to appear as a failure to keep pace with the demands of the newly emerging technological world. Industry and the universities required people with a better training in German and a

---

11. *Erlebtes Leben* (Frankfurt/M, 1928), p. 66.
12. *Der Deutsche und seine Schule* (Berlin, 1906), Chapter: "Wie ich erzogen wurde."

more thorough preparation in the mathematical-scientific disciplines than the tradition-bound humanistic Gymnasium could provide.

Attempts at reforming the system ensued in 1892 and 1900, on the latter occasion actively supported by Emperor Wilhelm II, who from his own unhappy experience had derived a strong dislike of the Gymnasium. No significant practical results were achieved, mainly because the obvious prerequisite for an extension of the curriculum in other directions, namely the reduction of the philological training, was prevented by reactionary forces within the schools and the civil service's continued insistence on this type of background for its recruits. The official exertions thus had the negative effect of still more overburdening the already hard-pressed pupils by leading to additions to the curriculum without compensating reductions. Added to the unwholesome and oppressive atmosphere which pervaded the secondary schools, this increase in their load drove many young people to despair. The result was an almost epidemic outbreak of suicides among high school pupils. Professor Gurlitt calculated that in the last twenty years of the nineteenth century no fewer than 1,152 adolescents thus took their own lives.[13]

But although the immediate cause for this tragic phenomenon lay in the educational sphere, the nature of the school as a prominent, representative aspect of the established adult society lent the pupils' suicides a much wider significance. Through their desperate act these young people demonstrated the enormous gap which had developed between their generation and the world of their parents. They felt that they could never fit into a world based on hypocrisy and double standards and—unlike the vast majority, which eventually adapted itself—saw no other way out than death.

Others neither compromised nor resorted to self-destruction, but found the strength to endure their bitter fate of loneliness and isolation. They became outcasts of a society based on such spurious foundations that it could not tolerate the scrutiny of spontaneously critical young minds. Among them were those who formed the expressionist movement.

13. Quoted in Robert Hessen, "Zur Hygiene des Schülerselbstmords," *Die Neue Rundschau* (September, 1911), p. 1295.

2. IN ZARATHUSTRA'S FOOTSTEPS

Loneliness, isolation, "outsidership"[1]—these are the central experiences in the life of the expressionists' generation. The biographies and works of authors usually regarded as expressionists stress these feelings consistently and unanimously, thus fully corroborating Wolfgang Paulsen's statement that the expressionist "um sein unabwendbares Schicksal der Vereinzelung weiss."[2]

Franz Werfel wrote in 1914, "eine entsetzliche *Einsamkeit* macht das Leben stumm,"[3] Ludwig Rubiner called "Isolation" and "Einzelner sein" the "Erbsünde" of the expressionists.[4] In many instances the outsidership is manifest in the restless, aimless peregrinations of the authors concerned. Theodor Däubler, who on his own evidence had a lonely childhood, led a wandering life from his adolescence until his death.[5] Carl Sternheim roamed through Europe from the turn of the century until he died in 1942.[6] René Schickele is called a "déraciné" in Barrès' sense by Ferdinand Lion, who furthermore compares Schickele's journalistic sojourn in Paris with Heine's exile.[7] Iwan Goll's autobiographical note in *Menschheitsdämmerung* reads: "Iwan Goll hat keine Heimat: durch Schicksal Jude, durch Zufall in Frankreich geboren, durch ein Stempelpapier als Deutscher bezeichnet." Alfred Ehrenstein, who led an irregular life and traveled a very great deal, suffered from an overpowering sense of loneliness which he vainly tried to overcome.[8] Alfred

---

1. This term will be used to refer to the estrangement of the expressionists from society. The word "outsidership" also acknowledges the expressionists' own adoption of the English word "outsider" to convey a graphic, accurate impression of their social situation.
2. *Expressionismus und Aktivismus. Eine typologische Untersuchung* (Bern, 1935), p. 164.
3. "Aphorismus zu diesem Jahr," *Die Aktion* (1914), cols. 48-49, from the photomechanical reprint (Stuttgart, 1961).
4. "Der Kampf mit dem Engel," *Die Aktion* (1917), cols. 16-17.
5. See Theodor Däubler, *Dichtungen und Schriften,* ed. F. Kemp (München, 1956), p. 866; see also the biographical note on Däubler in *Menschheitsdämmerung.*
6. Carol Petersen, "Carl Sternheim," in *Expressionismus. Gestalten einer literarischen Bewegung,* ed. Hermann Friedmann and Otto Mann (Heidelberg, 1956), p. 281.
7. "René Schickele," in Friedmann and Mann, p. 205.
8. See *Menschheitsdämmerung,* biographical note; Albert Soergel, *Dichtung*

Wolfenstein is called "ein Einsamer" by Carl Mumm, who uses terms like "Wirklichkeitsverlust," "Kontaktverlust" and "radikale Isolierung" to describe Wolfenstein's position in the world.[9] Georg Trakl's relations with his surroundings were marked by mutual incomprehension, so that he felt nowhere at home, neither in the sphere of his family, nor, on a different level, in his own time whose rabid materialism he blamed for his fate.[10]

"Ich bin der ferne, der schmerzliche Outsider," declares the poet in *Die Versuchung* by Franz Werfel, to whom Fritz Martini ascribes "quälende Einsamkeit."[11] Franz Kafka, like Werfel from Prague, was a particularly exemplary case of loneliness. Besides his most unsatisfactory relationship with his father and his Jewish environment, the fact that he lived outside Germany proper contributed to his tormenting outsidership. "Zu seiner Situation als germanisierter Prager Jude gehörte, dass er zwar deutsch sprach und schrieb, aber, von den Quellen der deutschen Sprache abgeschnitten, zur sprachlichen Urschöpfung gar nicht imstande war, und dass ihm auch darin sein Ausgestossensein bewusst wurde."[12]

As the names mentioned above indicate, the virulent anti-semitism, intensifying in the Jewish youths a feeling of ostracism, caused them to play a disproportionately large role in the expressionist movement. Whereas the Jews accounted for less than 1 per cent of the total German population, they made up more than 30 per cent of the contributors to *Menschheitsdämmerung*. In Karl Otten's anthology of expressionistic prose *Ahnung und Aufbruch*, the ratio is even higher: 21 out of 51 contributors.[13]

In Germany anti-semitic tendencies were, to be sure, based on old traditions, but their intensity was determined by contemporary conditions. This is recognized in the most frequently advanced explanation for the emergence of a strong anti-semitic current in the latter half of the

---

und Dichter der Zeit. Neue Folge. Im Banne des Expressionismus (Leipzig, 1925), p. 457; Edgar Lohner's introduction to "Die Lyrik des Expressionismus," Part I of Friedmann and Mann.

9. *Alfred Wolfenstein. Eine Einführung in sein Werk und eine Auswahl,* in the series "Verschollene und Vergessene" (Wiesbaden, 1955), pp. 5 ff.

10. See Helmut Uhlig, "Vom Ästhetizismus zum Expressionismus: Ernst Stadler, Georg Heym und Georg Trakl," in Friedmann and Mann, pp. 107-8; Fritz Martini, *Was war Expressionismus?* (Urach, 1948), p. 114.

11. *Die Versuchung,* in Karl Otten, *Schrei und Bekenntnis. Expressionistisches Theater* (Darmstadt, 1959), p. 634; Martini, *Was war Expressionismus?* p. 136.

12. Walter Muschg, *Von Trakl zu Brecht* (München, 1961), p. 81.

13. *Ahnung und Aufbruch,* p. 38.

nineteenth century. According to this view, in the old forms of society the Jews had faced the boycott of the tradesmen's guilds and other professional groups and were thus, as it were, predestined to invade the "free" professions of lawyer, journalist, financier, and others, when these under the new conditions gained in importance. As the non-Jewish citizens, whose previously protective organizations now became hindrances in the race to adapt themselves to the changing times, noted the advantages which in this respect the untrammeled Jews had over them, a powerful stimulus for anti-semitic feelings was given.[14]

However, the still often reiterated idea that in a sense the Jews provoked feelings of hatred from the rest of the population by monopolizing enterprises such as journalism is not based on facts. "In der gesamten Linkspresse, die als total verjudet galt, waren von 400 Redakteuren noch nicht zwanzig jüdisch, so dass selbst dort der fragwürdigen Idee proportionaler Gerechtigkeit Genüge getan war."[15]

Nor does the notion that the Jews as a group were enemies of the state and politically dangerously progressive stand up under an examination of the facts. It is therefore likely that the basic cause of the virulent anti-semitism of the era was to be found in hidden psychological processes, which conscious reasons only served to disguise. Harry Pross suggests that the disintegration of the traditional social order had destroyed the old set of class-bound standards, and had left especially the bourgeoisie, whose role in society the changes had most drastically affected, without any authoritative philosophy of life. The fluidity of modern society exposed them to equalizing tendencies—they grossly overestimated the extent— and thus made them susceptible to the ideological scale of values represented by racial discrimination. These tendencies were exploited by unscrupulous writers like H. Naudh, W. Marr, W. Stapel, A. Bartels, Th. Fritsch and also the later H. v. Treitschke,[16] and by certain political organizations such as the *Alldeutscher Verband* and the *Christlich-soziale Partei*. To make their anti-semitic propaganda more effective, it was given a pseudo-scientific or pseudo-religious foundation, which led to the inflation of such vague notions as "Rasse" and "Volk."

The tone and level on which these anti-semitic campaigns were conducted may be exemplified by a quotation from one of a series of articles

---

14. See Theobald Ziegler, *Die geistigen und sozialen Strömungen,* Chapter: "Der Antisemitismus."

15. *Die Zerstörung der deutschen Politik. Dokumente 1871-1933,* ed. Harry Pross (Hamburg, Frankfurt/M, 1959), p. 242.

16. *Ibid.,* Chapter VI, "Antisemitismus."

18

which in the years 1876 to 1878 appeared in the periodical which is rightly regarded as a symbol of the Wilhelmian bourgeoisie, the *Gartenlaube*. Under the title "Nicht länger Toleranz," the typical article reads as follows:

Nicht länger dürfen falsche Toleranz und Sentimentalität, leidige Schwäche und Furcht uns Christen abhalten, gegen die Auswüchse, Ausschreitungen und Anmassungen der Judenschaft vorzugehen. Nicht länger dürfen wir's dulden, dass die Juden überall die Führung, das grosse Wort an sich reissen. Sie schieben uns Christen stets beiseite, sie drücken uns an die Wand, sie nehmen uns die Luft und den Atem. Sie führen tatsächlich die Herrschaft über uns; sie besitzen eine gefährliche Übermacht, und sie üben einen höchst unheilvollen Einfluss. Seit vielen Jahrhunderten ist es wieder zum erstenmal, dass ein fremder, an Zahl so kleiner Stamm die grosse eigentliche Nation beherrscht. Die ganze Weltgeschichte kennt kein zweites Beispiel, dass ein heimatloses Volk, eine physisch wie psychisch entschieden degenerierte Rasse, bloss durch List und Schlauheit, durch Wucher und Schacher, über den Erdkreis gebietet.[17]

This venomous tirade leaves no doubt about the wide gulf of misunderstanding and hatred which separated the average Wilhelmian middle-class citizen and "subject" from his Jewish compatriots.[18]

In very many works of the expressionist generation, human isolation occurs as a leading motif. Walter Sokel cites instances from the works of Johst, Werfel, Frank, Kornfeld, Sack, Trakl, and Wolfenstein—to mention only some of those who are generally regarded as expressionists.[19] The first comprehensive study on Georg Heym drew attention to the obvious preoccupation with peripheral human beings in his poetry.[20] In the mad, sick, crippled and maimed, Heym reduced the involved and often intangible factors leading to the isolation of the expressionists to the concrete level of physical or mental deficiency. Georg Kaiser points to the creative activity of the poet as a stigma which separates him from his brethren. "Namen und Werk—richtet nicht diese Wand zwischen euch und mich auf. Sind wir nicht Brüder? . . . Stosst mich nicht aus. Ver-

17. Otto Glagau, "Der Börsen—und Gründungsschwindel" (1876), quoted in *Die Zerstörung der deutschen Politik*, p. 253.
18. Comparable to Jewish descent as a factor aggravating the outsidership of many expressionists was the international family background of writers such as Heinrich Mann and Gottfried Benn. See Sokel, *The Writer in Extremis*, n17, p. 180.
19. *Ibid.*, Chapters: "Poeta dolorosus," and "The Impotence of the Heart."
20. Helmut Greulich, *Georg Heym 1887-1912. Leben und Werk* (Berlin, 1931), Chapter: "Das Lebensgefühl in den Dichtungen."

langt nicht das Werk von mir. Zeichnet mich nicht mit eisigem Namen."[21]

This isolation and loneliness of the expressionist artists must be distinguished from the "schicksalhaft-notwendige natürliche Einsamkeit des Unverstandenseins grosser echter Kunst und Tat," from the "absolute Einsamkeit des dämonisch-schöpferischen Menschen."[22] The latter, as the natural consequence of the truly great creative mind's uniqueness among men, occurs where and whenever genius is found.

The outsidership of the expressionists, on the other hand, was not part of a timeless and universal problem, but an aspect of the gradually deepening individualism of Western man.[23] As a historically determined phenomenon, it continued a trend which made itself felt for the first time in the romantic era, when an entire movement consisting of greater and lesser talents—by no means all "geniuses"—was characterized by a consciously experienced outsidership. "Es ist die romantische und spätromantische Generation, die dies bis zur Furchtbarkeit erlebt, die zuerst die zerrissene, problematische Natur und Existenz, das forcierte Talent darstellt und erlebt und aus ihrem Ich und Ichkult nicht mehr den so ersehnten Weg in die Gemeinschaft findet. . . . Tieck, in seiner labilen, nervösen Verfassung deutliches Beispiel für die entbundene, fessellos romantische Existenz und gerade in seiner Jugend oft und plötzlich von dem Wissen letzter Einsamkeit unter den Menschen lähmend befallen, bekennt: 'Wir leben jeder einsam für sich, und keiner vernimmt den andern.' Die Dichtung der Zeit, die Brentanos, Hofmanns, Tiecks, Wetzels, zeigt dann diese neuen umherirrenden, mitten unter den Menschen gespenstisch einsamen Menschen."[24]

Particularly tragic was the fate of those men of genius in whom both types of loneliness seem to be combined. Possibly the earliest of these was Heinrich von Kleist, in whose works the figure of the outsider occurs in various guises, most clearly in that of Michael Kohlhaas, subtler in Friedrich von Homburg.[25] Clearly, Kleist's preoccupation with such figures as Kohlhaas and Homburg reflects the central problem of his own existence. His life was one desperate struggle to come to terms with the world, and its ultimate failure left him no choice but to commit suicide. Walter Silz confirms the belief that it was Kleist's human situation which drove him

---

21. *Die Erneuerung. Skizze für ein Drama,* in Karl Otten, *Schrei und Bekenntnis,* p. 54.
22. Walther Rehm, "Der Dichter und die neue Einsamkeit," *Zeitschrift für Deutschkunde,* XLV (1931), 548. 23. *Ibid.,* pp. 545-46. 24. *Ibid.,* pp. 549-50.
25. See Walter Silz, *Heinrich von Kleist* (Philadelphia, 1961), p. 232.

to the fatal step. "It was not the failure of his poetic genius that drove him to suicide. . . . But it was the man rather than the poet who called a halt. . . . The tormented man destroyed himself and in so doing destroyed the poet and all his unwritten works."[26]

Georg Heym's diaries indicate that the outsider position of the expressionists gave them a strong feeling of spiritual kinship with Heinrich von Kleist.[27] As far as his actual influence was concerned, however, Kleist was of much less importance for the expressionists than the figure in whom the tragic loneliness and isolation of the modern artist found its absolute climax: Friedrich Nietzsche.

Though the Nietzschean spirit began to be a factor of importance in the neo-romantic and neo-classicist currents around the turn of the century, its full impact was not felt until Heym's generation. In 1888, in the first book of *Umwertung aller Werte*, Nietzsche himself had prophesied: "Dies Buch gehört den Wenigsten. Vielleicht lebt noch Keiner von ihnen. Es mögen Die sein, welche meinen Zarathustra verstehn: wie *dürfte* ich mich mit Denen verwechseln, für welche heute schon Ohren wachsen?—Erst das Übermorgen gehört mir. Einige werden posthum geboren."[28] Walter Muschg confirms the hypothesis that only in the expressionist era had Nietzsche's time really come. "Nietzsches Abrechnung mit der europäischen Zivilisation begann erst jetzt als Sprengstoff zu wirken."[29]

Nietzsche represented the ideal type of charismatic leader whose personality is a suitable object both for veneration and for identification. It is this personality and its poetic idealization in Zarathustra which—apart from his unorthodox treatment of the German language—had the greatest influence on the expressionist generation. The effect was, however, most ambiguous. On the one hand Nietzsche, through his own fate of insanity even more than through his utterances on the subject, convinced the expressionists that their creative activity was, in the final analysis, the outcome and manifestation of a personality defect. As Walther Rehm declares, "Nietzsche ist es, der . . . dem modernen künstlerischen Menschen mit untrüglichem psychologischem Spürsinn und der schmerzhaften Erkenntnis eigenen Betroffenseins die Larve abreisst und ihn in seiner Lebensohnmacht vor aller Augen durchleuchtet, ihn grausam blosz-

---

26. *Ibid.*, pp. 286-87.
27. See diary entries: 10.21.1907; 2.10.1908; 7.20.1909; 12.10.1911, in Georg Heym, *Dichtungen und Schriften, Gesamtausgabe,* Vol. III: *Tagebücher Träume Briefe,* ed. Karl Ludwig Schneider (Hamburg, München, 1960).
28. *Nietzsches Werke* (Leipzig, 1896), Part I, Vol. VIII, p. 215.
29. *Von Trakl zu Brecht* (München, 1961), pp. 32-33.

stellt und den tiefsten, verborgensten Gründen seiner Lebenshaltung nachgeht. . . . Er fasst den Künstler als den pathologischen Menschen schlechthin und sieht in dieser pathologischen Verfassung geradezu die Bedingung des Schaffens."[30]

Around the turn of the century, Nietzsche's view was lent added weight by the theories of Sigmund Freud, who likewise stressed the pathological basis of the arts, which he designated as "Ersatzbefriedigungen."[31] The impact of these notions on the minds of the expressionists can be gauged from their works, about which Walter Sokel remarks in this context, "A deep conviction of unworthiness runs as a constant theme through the works of the Expressionists. In fact, Expressionism can be viewed as the attempt of a generation to come to grips with and somehow transcend the calamitous self-contempt that has overtaken the modern poet."[32]

Whereas Nietzsche contributed much to the "inferiority complex" which burdened the expressionists, on the other hand, he showed them the way to conquer it, or at least to give their isolation a purpose. He may therefore be regarded as the source of the ambivalent attitude of the expressionists towards the rank-and-file citizen whom they envied for his sense of belonging and his supposedly robust personality, and at the same time despised for his narrow-minded, materialistic outlook on the world. "The Expressionist artist not only feels superior to the average man, but he also feels inferior to him."[33]

The ambivalence which marked the expressionist's personal attitude towards the individual Wilhelmian bourgeois also affected his view of the existing society. In this case the development of such mixed feelings was stimulated by the demands of everyday existence. In daily life the Wilhelmian world could not be disdainfully renounced in its entirety.

---

30. "Der Dichter und die neue Einsamkeit," p. 556. The view of some romantics that literary creation as an occupation represented an abnormal disruption of the natural harmony between man's faculties, and therefore was something to be somewhat ashamed of, already points the way to Nietzsche's much more drastic notions. See, for instance, Clemens Brentano's *Geschichte vom braven Kasperl und dem schönen Annerl:* "Mein Herr, ein jeder Mensch hat, wie Hirn, Herz, Magen, Milz, Leber und dergleichen, auch eine Poesie im Leibe; wer aber eines dieser Glieder überfüttert, verfüttert oder mästet und es über alle andre hinüber treibt, ja es gar zum Erwerbzweig macht, der muss sich schämen vor seinem ganzen übrigen Menschen. Einer, der von der Poesie lebt, hat das Gleichgewicht verloren, und eine übergrosse Gänseleber, sie mag noch so gut schmecken, setzt doch immer eine kranke Gans voraus." *Brentanos Werke,* ed. Max Preitz (Leipzig, Wien, 1914), I, 353.

31. *Das Unbehagen in der Kultur* (Frankfurt/M, Hamburg, 1953), Chapter 2.   32. *The Writer in Extremis,* p. 83.   33. *Ibid.,* p. 82.

The expressionists had to compromise with its traditions when it came to attending the university, making a living, trying to gain a modicum of human happiness. Moreover, they could not fail to be to some extent and in some respects affected in their ideas and opinions by the atmosphere in which they grew up. After all, the historical perspective which yields a negative image of Wilhelmian Germany as a whole does not do justice to the enthusiasm technological progress can inspire, regardless of its ideological background, nor to the timeless capacity of humans for finding happiness in each other.

Nietzsche exerted a positive, encouraging influence on the minds of the youth of the later Wilhelmian period by providing their isolated existence with an aim and a purpose. This can be seen in a diary note in which the eighteen-year-old Georg Heym wrote, "Seine Lehre ist gross. Was man dagegen sagen mag, sie giebt unserm Leben einen neuen Sinn. . . . Ferner und ferner sehen lernen, sich wegwenden vom Augenblick und dem Übermenschen zu leben, lehrt uns Zarathustra. Und diese Lehre kann uns auf uns allein stellen."[34] It is important that Heym in these words proves that the basic tenets of Nietzsche's ideas were absorbed even by those who possessed neither the mental maturity nor the training necessary for a full appreciation of his philosophy. And it was not only the principle of *amor fati* which became part of the outlook on life of Heym and his compeers. In the same note Georg Heym quoted his favorite passage from *Zarathustra* which, significantly, is the one commencing with the lines, "Neues will ein Edler schaffen,/Und eine neue Tugend." By his preference Heym manifested how tempting the idea of an "Umwertung aller Werte" and a new order was even to those of the expressionist generation who knew Nietzsche as an artist rather than as a philosopher.

It is the Nietzschean element in the expressionists' work that accounts for the characteristic differences which set it apart from that of other lonely, isolated, ostracized writers. Hitherto, the traditional fundamental values attributed to life had never really been seriously and concertedly challenged. Even those artists who could not conform to the prevailing codices, and as a consequence were forced into an outsider position, had by and large accepted the views of the community as the norm and their own as an anomaly.

The attitude of the community being regarded as fixed and immutable, the artist's non-conformity with the established pattern became the object of his concern and creative activity. The egocentricity of the romantics appears, from this viewpoint, as a preoccupation with the

34. Diary note of 2.17.1906.

question why, and how, they deviated from the general standard.[35] They measured themselves by the world's yard-stick, whereas the expressionists reversed the process and applied their own standard to the values of their environment. From this self-centered perspective the expressionists' criticism derived a unique degree of uncompromising finality and conviction.

Another factor also contributed to lend the expressionist opposition an unprecedented significance. When the pre-expressionist author attacked, provoked, or ridiculed the bourgeoisie, even when he did not limit himself to certain sectors such as the Kleinstädter, his action affected only a relatively unimportant and uninfluential part of the community. Thus the bourgeois writer who, for whatever reasons, bore a grudge against his class could expose all its vices and idiosyncrasies without upsetting the principles and values on which the life of the people as a whole was based.

In Wilhelmian Germany, owing to the social reorganization which had accompanied the industrial revolution, the bourgeoisie had achieved a position of great predominance, and had put its stamp on every aspect of life in the empire. Thus to the expressionist the bourgeois stratum from which he hailed *was* the state, and in questioning the world view prevailing in his environment he put in doubt the order of the universe.[36]

35. Cf. Rehm, "Der Dichter und die neue Einsamkeit," p. 549.
36. See Kuno Brombacher, *Der deutsche Bürger im Literaturspiegel von Lessing bis Sternheim* (München, 1920).

3. EXPRESSIONISTS
AND EXPRESSIONISM

The ambivalent feelings with which the expressionists from their position on the periphery of society regarded their fellow citizens determined the expressionist world view. Their feeling of hostility towards the community from which they were excluded, and whose values they had recognized as spurious, accounts for the critical outlook which became their most striking common characteristic. As Fritz Martini declares, "Die alles aufregende, noch heute keineswegs nur historisch gewordene Wirkung der expressionistischen Bewegung lag darin, dass sie rücksichtslos alles Gegebene, Bestehende, Überlieferte in Frage stellte, alle verbürgten, scheinbar endgültigen Ordnungen umwarf und durchstrich."[1]

At the same time, however, the positive side of their ambivalent feelings concerning society and the natural reaction to their loneliness and torturing isolation caused them to go beyond a purely negative attitude toward the existing state of affairs. Opposition to the status quo was not their only aim; they were also—at least potentially—inspired by some view or concept of a better world which was to take the place of the Wilhelmian reality they rejected.

These two notions gave the expressionists the urge to destroy symbolically the world and authority of the "fathers," not as a nihilistic end in itself, but in order to pave the way for a better, higher form of life. The desired destruction of the existing order was, in other words, a purgatory act with which the messianic expressionist wanted to prepare mankind for the advent of a superior pattern of existence. With reference to the inter-generation tension in which the position of the expressionists generally manifested itself, it could be said that they did not just want to kill their fathers to be rid of them; they wanted to raise them to a higher plane of humanity. The expressionists were not nihilists, but wanted the authority to which they were subjected to be worthy of their respect and reverence.

Among the expressionists there were, however, vast differences in the relative importance which they assigned to the destruction of the old world and to the creation of a new one. At one end of the scale there were those who really had no clear conception of what should replace the existing pattern of life. They were almost completely engrossed by the

1. *Was war Expressionismus?* p. 23.

idea of the prerequisite demolition of the established order, and what lay beyond it occurred to them at best in occasional, almost fleeting prospects of undefined and unspecified serenity or felicity. An extreme instance of this negative outlook is that of Georg Heym, as appears from such well-known diary entries as "Warum ermordet man nicht den Kaiser oder den Zaren? Man lässt sie ruhig weiter schädlich sein. Warum macht man keine Revolution? . . . Würden einmal wieder Barrikaden gebaut. Ich wäre der erste, der sich darauf stellte, ich wollte noch mit der Kugel im Herzen den Rausch der Begeisterung spüren."[2]

In contrast to such predominantly "negative" expressionists there were those who acknowledged the need of overthrowing the Establishment as an inevitable preparatory step, but focussed their attention mainly on the new world they wanted to establish on the ruins of the old.

These writers can be divided into two major categories depending upon the nature of their ideal world image. First, there were those who envisaged the future in terms of a society reorganized along definite political lines, invariably based on a communist or socialist ideology. Ernst Toller provides an example of this type of expressionist who saw the salvation of mankind in the replacement of the existing social order by a different one. A brief survey of his activities during the latter part of the war and the subsequent revolutionary days reads, "Organisiert mit Kurt Eisner den Widerstand gegen den Krieg. Beteiligt am Streik der Munitionsarbeiter in München 1918. Verhaftet, im November freigelassen. Vorsitzender der Arbeiter-, Bauern- und Soldatenräte in München. Spielte eine führende Rolle in der bayerischen Räterepublik 1919. Im Juni 1919 verhaftet, zu 5 Jahren Festung verurteilt."[3]

Second, there was a group that pinned its hopes, not on a reorganization of society, but on the intrinsic qualities of the human soul. These writers were convinced of mankind's innate goodness, which they considered to be restrained and prevented from asserting itself by the strait jacket of objectionable social codes and conventions into which the individual was forced. They visualized the redemption of man as a liberation of the elemental forces which he harbored in his soul. If the social compulsion which kept these potential spiritual powers in bondage could in any way whatever be overcome, all mankind would be united in universal love. A feeling of brotherhood would draw all men into one

2. *Dichtungen und Schriften,* III, 135, 139.
3. Catalogue No. 7, *Expressionismus. Literatur und Kunst 1910-1923,* of the Schiller-Nationalmuseum, Marbach a.N., published by Bernhard Zeller for the Deutsche Schillergesellschaft on the occasion of the "Sonderausstellung" from May 8 till October 31, 1960, p. 314.

happy community without barriers or discriminations. Any social organization whatever would, of course, constitute a serious obstacle on the road toward such a blissful state of humane anarchy.

Those who embraced as their ideal the establishment of a new world founded solely on the hypothesis that man is basically good tended therefore to deviate somewhat from the other types of expressionist in their attitude towards the Establishment. Whereas both the negativistic and the political expressionists opposed the specific form of social organization found in Middle Europe at the beginning of the modern technological age, the "anarchists" were inclined to reject the idea of society as such, thereby rising to some extent above the very subjective and limited perspective of the others. René Schickele exemplifies the type of expressionist who passionately believes that man is good, when, with an allusion to Novalis, (which in itself is significant) he associates the emergence of a new, liberated humanity with the unveiling of the statue of Sais. "Ein Gesicht erscheint im Atmosphärenwust der Angst und Lüge: das Gesicht des Menschen. Das Gesicht einer Kreatur, überirdisch glänzend."[4]

In spite of their divergent formulations of the basic expressionist attitude *against* the old order and in *favor* of a new ideal, expressionist writers from all three groups shared one fundamental desire. They all wanted to bring about certain changes in the world which would make it conform to their own standards, so that they might be delivered from their outsidership and be integrated in the community. And this reformation of reality was to be achieved by means of their writing; their creative activity was intended to bring about the downfall of the old and the establishment of a new pattern of existence.

Their writing was not to be a record of their private ideas, not the immediate embodiment of mental processes based on the poet's emotional experience in a symbolic form which requires the reader's sympathetic understanding and initiative in order to be intelligible. The expressionists wanted to break through their isolation and establish contact with their fellows; they were driven by the desire to affect them and their outlook on the world. Therefore they addressed their work to a public which was to be forcefully called to attention and influenced.

This rhetorical approach manifested itself in general in the large number of periodicals and broadsheets published by the expressionists and in the activities of the numerous cabarets. Among the latter the Neopathetische Cabaret in Berlin played a particularly important part in the

4. Quoted in Soergel and Hohoff, p. 127.

27

emergence of the early expressionist movement. It was an enterprise of the equally important Neue Club, founded in March, 1909, by Kurt Hiller, which counted Georg Heym, Jakob van Hoddis, and Ernst Blass among its most creatively gifted members.[5]

The expressionists' tendency to use their creative talent to gain the ear of their fellow citizens and, above all, influence them in their ideas and their way of living is programmatically expressed in the opening lines of Johannes R. Becher's *Vorbereitung*:

> Der Dichter meidet strahlende Akkorde.
> Er stösst durch Tuben, peitscht die Trommel schrill.
> Er reisst das Volk auf mit gehackten Sätzen.[6]

Even more explicit in this respect is the speech with which Kurt Hiller, in October, 1912, introduced his literary Cabaret Gnu:

> Meine Herren, meine Damen!
> Sie erwarten jetzt Sätze zu hören über den sogenannten Zweck dieses Cabarets. Mit dem, was Sie sich selber sagen können, möchte ich Sie nicht langweilen: nämlich damit, dass hier eine junge Gruppe von Litteraten durch Gesprochnes die Wirkung verstärken will, die ihr das bloss Geschriebne, infolge der Schlechtigkeit oder Abhängigkeit fast aller Journale, in nur schwachem Grade bietet. . . . Verlogen oder sehr dumm ist ein Künstler, stellt er in Abrede, dass sein Tun, das blosse Kunst-Schaffen, bereits ein Mittel sei, Macht über Gemüter (und nicht nur über Gemüter!) zu gewinnen.[7]

Otto Mann summarizes the aspirations of the expressionists when he describes their attitude in the words: "Es soll wieder eine wirkungsmächtigere Kunst geschaffen werden."[8]

Thus it is clear that the expressionists strove for persuasive, efficacious literary expression of their unhappy outsidership and consequent am-

---

5. In June, 1910, the Neopathetische Cabaret presented the first of its programs, which consisted of recitations, lectures on philosophical, political, and other themes, and performances of contemporary music. Unfortunately, less than one year after its inception, the development of this most significant venture was halted prematurely when a schism occurred in the Neue Club, and left it bereft of its organizer and key figure Kurt Hiller. The death of Georg Heym in January, 1912, dealt a fatal blow to both organizations, which dissolved soon afterwards. For a detailed account of the rise and fall of the Neue Club and the Neopathetische Cabaret, see my article, "Georg Heym und der Neue Club," *Revista de Letras* (Assis), IV (1963), 262-71.

6. Unless otherwise specified, all quotations of expressionist poetry are from *Menschheitsdämmerung,* with the exception of Georg Heym's poems, which are quoted after *Gesammelte Gedichte,* ed. Carl Seelig (Zürich, 1947).

7. Hiller, *Die Weisheit der Langenweile, eine Zeit- und Streitschrift* (Leipzig, 1913), I, 239-40.   8. Friedmann and Mann, p. 23.

bivalent attitude towards society. Their world image's fundamental polarity, with Establishment and ideal as the respective objects of their hatred and yearning, appeared on the individual level either as all-absorbing hostility toward established values and concepts, or as preoccupation with the new world which was to rise out of the ruins of the old. The positive ideal could either be of a socio-political nature, or be envisaged as a state of happy anarchy based only on man's supposed inherent goodness.

The three types of attitude found among the expressionists are reflected in expressionist writing, which can be analogously divided into three groups. Depending upon the peculiar nature of the individual talents, each of these subdivisions in itself includes a variety of techniques and approaches. In spite of such differences in execution, all literature which is traditionally regarded as undoubtedly expressionist displays one of three possible attitudes. Corresponding to the three types of mental attitude, expressionist writing either fanatically attacks the status quo, giving only incidental and unspecified glimpses of a better world, or it evokes visions of an ideal community without dwelling on the necessity to overcome the old order first. The ideal itself can be a new social organization, or an anarchic brotherhood of men based only on mutual love.

It should perhaps be stressed that the three types and the three literary patterns so described are theoretical constructions representing the extremes of a sliding scale. "Pure" types are rare; it is the predominance of traits belonging to one type over those pertaining to others which is decisive. Even with the latter reservation, one can ascribe a type only to individual pieces of writing, not collectively to the work of an author who may change his mind or be subject to emotions which temporarily color his views. In most cases there is likely to be a large degree of consistency in the writings of one person, especially over a limited period of time; however, the exceptions are too numerous to ignore.

For the following interpretations which will demonstrate the three patterns of expressionist writing, texts have been selected which, each in its own way, are unambiguously representative of a particular trend. First those works are to be considered in which negative, destructive criticism of the existing state of affairs is the predominant feature, while positive aspects play a minimal role and are represented only in isolated, unspecific allusions to a better world. In the general objurgatory atmosphere which by their very nature pervades such writings, the idealistic elements are very frequently couched in an ironical tone. Often, too, the unattainability of the ideal is implied, thus strengthening the pessimistic

29

portent of the work, or else the author did no more than introduce a fleeting vision of serenity into an otherwise ugly and repulsive scene. In spite of such qualifying circumstances, the presence of positive traits, no matter how slight or in what context, hints at the existence of the possibility of an ideal.

Among exponents of this current, one could mention Gustav Sack, for instance in his poem *Bagatelle* which gives a very negative picture of the big city as the epitome of the beginning technological era.

> In eine neue Bude zog ich ein!
> Ein schiefer Tisch, ein krummer Stuhl,
> eines wackligen Bettes Unzuchtpfuhl —
> in diese Bude zog ich ein.
>
> Garküchen unter mir und Kegelbahnen,
> mir gegenüber 'ne verdreckte Wand
> und über mir ein kleines blaues Band
> mit feinen weissen Wolkenfahnen.
>
> Was soll ich hier? Was will, was kann ich hier?
> Doch so war's immer schon:
> Armut und Dreck und wie zum Hohn
> leuchtet ein Fetzen Himmel mir.[9]

In this poem the references to the blue sky, which relieve the sordidness of the work, symbolize the polarity of the author's world view. A similar antithesis is sometimes introduced by Georg Heym, in whose work the positive elements also play a very minor, but by no means negligible, role. His poetic technique for attacking the established order is, however, very different from Sack's references in *Bagatelle* to the less savory aspects of the big city.

In Heym's work the prevailing concept of life is denied and contradicted through the postulation of a viewpoint which differs radically from the generally accepted anthropocentric one. Heym created a universe in which man is not the supreme force whose rational powers can subjugate and use the whole of nature for his own purpose, i.e., progress in the materialistic sense. In his works a de-animated humanity, reduced to utter insignificance in the cosmic order, is the passive victim of a cruel and inexorable fate. This reversal of the current conception of the world can be traced throughout Heym's entire work, including poetry, drama,

9. *Gedichte. Die drei Reiter* (Hamburg, München, 1958), p. 39.

and prose.[10] It may here be illustrated with the aid of his best known poem *Der Krieg*. It describes the emergence of the demon of war out of his subterranean realm and his devastating progress over the earth, in the course of which the vulnerability and helplessness of humanity reveal themselves in its blind panic and unheroic, collective suffering and death. In the second and third stanzas of the poem, Heym depicts the shadow thrown ahead by the approaching catastrophe and shows how it casts a spell over the people, halting their movements and arousing fear and uncertainty in them.

> In den Abendlärm der Städte fällt es weit,
> Frost und Schatten einer fremden Dunkelheit.
> Und der Märkte runder Wirbel stockt zu Eis.
> Es wird still. Sie sehn sich um. Und keiner weiss.
>
> In den Gassen fasst es ihre Schulter leicht.
> Eine Frage. Keine Antwort. Ein Gesicht erbleicht.
> In der Ferne zittert ein Geläute dünn,
> Und die Bärte zittern um ihr spitzes Kinn.

The next quatrain begins with the lines:

> Auf den Bergen hebt er schon zu tanzen an,
> Und er schreit: "Ihr Krieger alle, auf und an!"

This summons to the warriors stresses the crucial fact about Heym's treatment of the subject matter: war is represented, not as an inter-human, but as a super-human phenomenon; it presses mankind into its service; man does not "make" war for his own purposes. The fate of those enlisted under the banners of war is death.

> Wo der Tag flieht, sind die Ströme schon voll Blut.
> Zahllos sind die Leichen schon im Schilf gestreckt,
> Von des Todes starken Vögeln weiss bedeckt.

No better lot than the warriors meet with awaits the fleeing civilians.

> Und was unten auf den Strassen wimmelnd flieht,
> Stösst er in die Feuerwälder, wo die Flamme brausend zieht.

10. See my article, "Georg Heyms *Der Dieb*—ein Novellenbuch?" in *Levende Talen*, No. 215 (June, 1962), pp. 352 ff; also my forthcoming book on Heym.

That there is no direct mention of the people, but only the derogatory reference to their swarming flight, is a characteristic indication of the wretched, victimized anonymity of these human lives. These visions of passive human suffering reach a climax in the next to last quatrain, with the collective annihilation of mankind in the collapsing, burning city.

> Eine grosse Stadt versank in gelbem Rauch,
> Warf sich lautlos in des Abgrunds Bauch.

The utter negativism and pessimism of Heym's world view as exemplified in this poem is, however, in a few cases relieved through the introduction of a final vision of serenity and beauty which seems to hold some hope for mankind by implying that there must be some escape from its plight. An example of this is the stanza which ends a depressing and dehumanized depiction of a *Laubenfest*:

> Im blauen Abend steht Gewölke weit,
> Delphinen mit den rosa Flossen gleich,
> Die schlafen in der Meere Einsamkeit.

The ideal which is only wistfully and indirectly alluded to in this category of expressionist literature forms the main theme of the other patterns of expressionism, in which the criticism and the poetic destruction of the existing world are an essential but subordinate preparation for the postulation of a utopian world image. As pointed out, in many cases the expressionist sees the salvation of mankind in the establishment of a new social order. The better world which these writers look forward to is seen as something to be consciously conceived and organized by themselves and their friends. The authors concerned play the parts of messianic agitators and reformers.

The first half of Reinhard Sorge's *Der Bettler,* one of the earliest dramas of the expressionist era, illustrates the pattern.[11] In this lyrical drama the denunciation of the status quo in its artistic and moral aspects takes place in the early scenes with the critics and prostitutes. Yet it amounts to a distortion of the facts when the play is characterized as an unmasking of the "Entartung des Gesellschafts- und Kulturlebens."[12]

This critical element forms by no means the substance of the work, but is merely a preparation for the visions of a new world. One of these stems from the young poet himself; the other from his insane father. The re-

11. Berlin, 1928.
12. Friedmann and Mann, p. 221.

32

lationship between these two figures is a very important factor in the play. Although there is mention of the fact that the poet is unhappy at home, Otto Mann misses the point when he states, "In Sorge's *Bettler* revoltiert der junge Dichter gegen ein bedrückendes Milieu."[13] Under the circumstances, the young poet's unhappiness about his environment is quite natural, and it only serves to motivate the Maecenas' offer of a stipend, the refusal of which leads the poet on to expound his utopian vision.

Far from posing a generation problem in the customary expressionist manner, the figure of the father introduces a variation on the son's theme of a better world to come. Each sees himself as the chosen redeemer of mankind, and takes upon himself the task of bringing about an improvement in the lot of humanity. This is very clearly expressed in the poet's words. "Ich will die Welt auf meine Schultern nehmen/Und sie mit Lobgesang zur Sonne tragen."

Walter Sokel points out the similarity which in this respect exists between father and son. "The Father constitutes a musical variation of the Messiah theme in *The Beggar*. His megalomaniacal Messianic dream functions as a counterpoint to the Son's search for meaning and salvation." But this commentator overemphasizes the father's materialism. "In contrast to the Son's idealism, the Father represents the materialistic counterpoint in the composition. He misinterprets the Messianic theme materialistically as technical progress and enrichment."[14]

That the father's vision goes beyond such narrow-minded materialism is indicated by his comparison of the sailing ships with doves. "Das sind die Tauben, die ich liebe." What he says about the bridges also shows that technical progress and riches are not his sole aim. "Oh Segen! Breite /Bruderbrücken binden Ufer und Ufer!/Ja, brüderlich!" In this context it is relevant that his vision concludes with the words: "Alle Wunder! Alle Wunder!" But the father's aim is best characterized by the striking similarity between his grandiose dream and the parts of *Faust II* in which the scene of Faust's final activities is described. The motifs of the canals which mean happiness, the ports, the ships, and the emphasis on the fertility of the transformed world, all occur in *Faust* in speeches by Philemon and Baucis,[15] Lynceus der Türmer,[16] and Faust himself.[17] The

---

13. Friedmann and Mann, p. 220.
14. *The Writer in Extremis*, p. 37.
15. Act V, "Offene Gegend."
16. Act V, "Palast."
17. Act V, "Grosser Vorhof des Palasts."

connection between the two works even extends to *der Weisheit letzter Schluss*: Faust's stress on the fact that man has to be diligent and brave in order to deserve the good life on his land, expressed in terms such as "kühn-emsig" and "tüchtig," is echoed in the father's line: "Ja, Segen! Brot und Mark schwankt in den Lüften." The same motifs occur in the young poet's vision. "Hungernde Mädchen,/Die um ihr unecht Kind sich mager mühen,/Sollen dort Brot finden." And somewhat later, "Männer aber/Sollen die Stirnen härten an Leid und Lust."

The difference between the two visions is one of accent only; the father concentrates on the development of the earth's resources as the source of the blessed, marvelous state of mankind his dream evokes, while the son hopes to achieve the same end through his own theater, which is to be "Das Herz der Kunst: aus allen Ländern strömen/Die Menschen alle an die heilige Stätte/Zur Heiligung, nicht nur ein kleines Häuflein/Erlesener!" This vision of a classless and international audience, which may well have been inspired by Wagner's original intentions for Bayreuth, provides the most specific socio-political symbol of Sorge's ideal of a better world to be found in this play.

Other authors in the socio-politically inclined form of expressionism had a more practical and realistic conception of the forces which shape society. An example may be found in Ernst Wilhelm Lotz' well known poem *Aufbruch der Jugend*. The first five stanzas conjure up visions of revolutionary turmoil and the forceful overthrow of the established order. The final quatrain then reads:

> Beglänzt von Morgen, wir sind die verheissnen Erhellten,
> Von jungen Messiaskronen das Haupthaar umzackt,
> Aus unsern Stirnen springen leuchtende, neue Welten,
> Erfüllung und Künftiges, Tage, sturmüberflaggt!

In these verses the poet represents the tradition of the self-proclaimed redeemer, which in this period was widely revived because of the authors' personal situation. Nailed on the cross by the world they lived in, they tried to comfort themselves by equating their fate with that of Christ. "The crucified is also the savior. Persecuted at present, he will inherit the kingdom of the elect. Those who scorn him now will one day throng to the theaters and museums to worship him."[18]

The drops of blood which the crown of thorns draws from their foreheads are the new worlds of the future, in which their ideas have found

18. *The Writer in Extremis*, p. 63.

fulfillment. This last image indicates not only the cerebral approach of the poet, but also the fact that he regards himself as the originator of a new order. In its extreme forms the approach represented by Lotz could lead to a disregard of artistic quality for the sake of political agitation, as can be observed in the works of such writers as Johannes R. Becher and Ludwig Rubiner.

Besides the negativistic and the socio-political trends, a third basic category is distinguishable in the realizations of the central expressionistic constellation of negative and positive concepts. It also emphasizes the latter, introducing destructive criticism of the established values and institutions only as a preliminary step to the establishment of a better society. This pattern presents the view that the faults inherent in the old order are to be overcome, not by organizing life in a new and better way, but by simply letting man's basic instincts guide him in a social vacuum. The writers stress the essential goodness of mankind, which, if only the influence of the existing order could be eliminated or overcome, would bring all men together in harmony and mutual love.

One such work is Carl Hauptmann's *Krieg. Ein Tedeum,* which de-picts the total destruction of established civilization and society in a war organized by the great powers and international finance. Afterwards, out of ruins and holes the cripples emerge, who, at first hesitantly, establish a relationship of mutual trust in spite of their national origin and social status in the old world. This new tentative atmosphere of universal brotherhood is subsequently confirmed in the emotional upsurge caused by the birth of the new man.[19]

The basic attitude from which these works sprang could also express itself in an entirely different manner. Thus a similar confidence in the essential goodness of mankind motivates Carl Sternheim's satirical play *Die Hose.*[20] In this so-called comedy the faults of the bourgeois world are illuminated through the contrast between those who have undergone its corroding influence on their personalities and the primitively vital Maske, who under the cloak of outward conformity has asserted his in-dependence of the stifling code. Sternheim, in attacking the middle-class world, shows that basically the bourgeois is a person of estimable quali-ties which are prevented from coming to the surface because of the un-propitious spirit of the age.

This interpretation of *Die Hose* deviates from the view held by Carol Petersen, who sees in the comedy an ironically exaggerated exposé of the

19. Text in Karl Otten, *Schrei und Bekenntnis,* pp. 126 ff.
20. *Die Hose. Ein bürgerliches Lustspiel,* 3rd ed. (München, 1920).

bourgeois vices as embodied in Maske. "In diesem Stück gab ein offenbar fanatischer Entlarver seinen Figuren etwas von seiner Kälte mit. . . . Der Dichter hatte sie stilisiert, liess ein Netz über sie werfen, in dem sie alle verzweifelt zappelten, ohne aus ihrer Umgarnung herauszukommen. Theobald Maske hiess der Mann, der dies Netz am gestreckten Arm hielt, selber eine überdimensionale Emanation niederer Begierden. Emporkommen, unbekümmert um Tränen und Opfer Getretener, schien der einzige Sinn seiner einträglichen Beatmung [sic]."[21]

This viewpoint oversimplifies the interrelationship of the characters; Maske's main counterpart Scarron, for instance, is not caught up in a net held by the other, but in his own "impotence of the heart."[22] When Luise offers herself to him, Theobald intervenes neither in the flesh nor in the spirit, and Scarron fails for no other reason than that love to him is only a word, not an emotion. Walter Sokel's opinion of *Die Hose* does take this circumstance into account, and avoids the error of seeing Maske as the ruthless Untermensch who demoniacally terrorizes the other characters. This commentator thus arrives at a more differentiated judgment on the bourgeois husband. "Crude and egotistical though he is, Maske can love. In contrast to the poet, who promises much and gives so little, the bourgeois promises little but accomplishes much."[23]

Scarron's reluctant admiration for the primitive manliness of Maske is, no doubt justifiably, interpreted by Sokel as an expression of Sternheim's own sentiments. Yet it appears that in the final assessment of the play Sokel, too, subscribes to the view that Sternheim's main aim is an attack on the figure of the middle-class citizen represented by Theobald Maske. "He secretly admires him while overtly attacking him."[24]

Apart from the fact that there is actually nothing secret about the admiration expressed for Maske in the play, the validity of this interpretation is further limited by the absence of any real criticism directed against him. Mandelstam and Scarron are not qualified to judge him, and their attacks against him end in their total defeat, while Gertrud Deuter, whose name is indicative of her function in this respect, radically changes her initially negative opinion of him after they have together examined the view from his bedroom window.

Sternheim's intentions with *Die Hose* have apparently always been subject to misunderstandings of this nature, for in the Foreword to the

21. "Carl Sternheim," in Friedmann and Mann, pp. 282-83.
22. Cf. Sokel, *Writer in Extremis*, Chapter 5: "The Impotence of the Heart," pp. 119 ff.
23. *Ibid.*, p. 123.
24. *Ibid.*

second edition he tried to correct them. According to Sternheim's own interpretation, borne out by the text, it is wrong to regard *Die Hose* as an ironical attack against the figure of Theobald Maske. The latter is not intended as a personification of the negative aspects of middle-class society. He is, on the contrary, an example with which the author intended to open the eyes of his bourgeois audience to their own fundamental virtues. Maske's basic qualities, such as the urges for self-preservation and for self-sufficiency which make him disregard literature and philosophy, are demonstrated to make him superior to the erudite Scarron and the latter's cheaper pendant Mandelstam.

These two are the main exponents of the bourgeois ideology in its various aspects; the barber, for instance, through his boundless admiration for the music of Wagner, who, at least in Sternheim's opinion, epitomized the worst aspects of the Zeitgeist.[25] As Mandelstam reveals himself through his enthusiasm for this composer, so does Scarron through the opinions he voices in the debate with Maske. The crassest example is his reaction when Theobald refers to the role of the heart. "Das Herz ist ein Muskel, Maske." It is Scarron, not Maske, who adheres to the pedestrian materialism which pervaded the mental atmosphere of Wilhelmian Germany. In his other utterances Scarron indulges in empty phraseology which is intended to sound profound, but really only covers up his unwillingness to face the concrete facts of life, such facts as "dass Frauen ein Herz haben, Kinder zur Welt kommen."

Another character who deliberately shuts out the world is the scholar Stengelhöh, who is usually disregarded in interpretations of *Die Hose*. He tries to arrange his life in such a way that he need not be reminded of the basic facts of sexuality, or of the existence of any living creatures such as small children, canaries, dogs, and cats. Maske, on the other hand, refuses to bother with the realms of science and the arts, and limits himself to the instinctual level of life. That level includes food and sex, but also an awareness of the nature of love and the ability to bring some happiness into the lives of his fellows.

The text of *Die Hose* thus justifies Sternheim's claims that he wanted

25. In *Berlin oder Juste Milieu* (München, 1920), pp. 36-37, he wrote: "Der Sachse Richard Wagner, von höheren Fügungen in seiner Weltanschauung überhaupt absehend, brachte anstatt des christlichen Himmels das alte Walhall mit seinen Bewohnern dem Publikum wieder nah, nach ihrer Kleidung und sonstigen Ansprüchen ungezwungene Wesen, in deren Götterhall es aber derart skandalös und spiessbürgerlich herging, dass der gewöhnliche Sterbliche sich vollends überzeugte, wo Leben der Himmlischen so erbärmlich beschränkt und abhängig sei, könne er wirklich mit seiner Preussisch-Berliner Freiheit zufrieden sein, und mit vollem Recht von einem Fortschritt durch Jahrhunderte trotzalledem sprechen."

37

to awaken the bourgeois' "Mut zu seiner menschlichen Ursprünglich-keit," by demolishing the "Wall verabredeter Ideologien, Gaswolken von Apotheosen, Schützengräbern von Metaphern" behind which the middle class pursued its petty money-making.[26] The portrayal of Maske serves to show the vast resources of vitality which the bourgeois unleashes in himself if he refuses to pay homage to the artistic, philosophical, and scholarly sacred cows of his environment and time, and discards professional ambitions. But this lonely rebellion against the prevailing system is only possible under the cover of outward conformism—hence Maske's name and his concern about the central incident of the play, which might have resulted in the loss of his protective anonymity. He says, "Meine Unscheinbarkeit ist die Tarnkappe, unter der ich meinen Neigungen, meiner innersten Natur frönen darf."

In the field of poetry the absolute belief in the essential goodness of human nature is represented, among others, by Iwan Goll. The first version of Goll's poem *Der Panamakanal* (1912) describes the emergence of a harmonious brotherhood of men out of the ruins of the old world. In the first section, subtitled *Die Arbeit,* the towns with their palaces and hovels and all other man-made evidence of inequality and suppression are razed. But the tenacity of the old order is shown in the laborers' inability to overcome the barriers between them of nationality and religion. Only when the canal is finally completed, and the connection between the oceans made, does the new world rise out of the chaos. There will be no hostility, but only love.

> Und wenn diese Tore sich öffnen werden,
> Wenn zwei feindliche Ozeane mit Gejubel sich küssen—
> Oh, dann müssen
> Alle Völker weinen auf Erden.

In the second part of the work, *Die Weihe,* this universal fraternization is symbolized in a number of images and is shown in its effect on the life of the people. The barriers of language, color, and custom have disappeared, and in the atmosphere of freedom which has replaced the old restrictive order even differences in individual temperament are overcome by the feeling of love and brotherhood which now unites all mankind.

Sentiments such as these inevitably led to the poetic invocation of the God who is Love, and therewith to the ecstatic religious tone of many

26. *Juste Milieu,* pp. 50-51.

works by Werfel, Unruh, Heynicke, the post-*Bettler* Sorge, and others. In them the problems and sorrows of human existence are an incomprehensible part of a higher plan, and are left to Him to solve by His divine grace which He imparts to all mankind.

> erwacht zu schöpferischen Glücksaufschwüngen,
> schiesst Gottes Blut, das einmal schon vergeblich rann,
> durch aller Menschen Herzen in Kometensprüngen....[27]

The development of a religious attitude out of a simply human boundless love for all mankind and faith in its essential goodness, no matter how obscured and perverted through a hypocritical and evil social organization, can be demonstrated most clearly in the case of Franz Werfel. He was no less violently opposed to the existing order than poets like Sack and Heym, but his confidence in the basic qualities of his fellow men was so great that he yearned to be one with them, regardless of the unpleasant features which the established pattern of life may have given them. He did not concentrate on the evocation of destructive visions, as Heym did, but envisaged a universal brotherhood which would reduce the barriers of status, religious organization, race, and all others to utter insignificance.

His fundamental attitude is expressed in the opening line of the poem *An den Leser.* "Mein einziger Wunsch ist, dir, o Mensch verwandt zu sein!" It appears, however, that his own desire, his own will power are inadequate to the task of establishing the longed-for intimate relationship with all men against the resistance of the existing order. Thus the poem ends with an implied admission of defeat in the subjunctive mood of the verses: "O, könnte es einmal geschehen,/Dass wir uns, Bruder, in die Arme fallen!"

The realization that mere good intentions are impotent led Werfel to the invocation of a superior power, through whose intermediary he hoped to achieve his aim of identifying himself with the whole of humanity. This approach inevitably resulted in work of a predominantly religious nature. Werfel's writings include a number of poems which represent this turn to God as a way of overcoming his human isolation. A case in point is his poem entitled *Ich bin ja noch ein Kind.* In contrast to his statement in *An den Leser* "ich habe alle Schicksale durchgemacht," the poet here disclaims all familiarity with the fate of those less naïve and fortunate than he.

27. Paul Zech, *Die neue Bergpredigt.*

> Ich bin gesund,
> Und weiss noch nicht, wie Greise rosten.
> Ich hielt mich nie an groben Pfosten,
> Wie Frauen in der schweren Stund'.

Subsequent stanzas serve to illustrate the writer's incapability of identifying himself with any human being in any walk of life. His unfulfilled desire for identification, however, extends much farther than the human realm to which *An den Leser* is limited. In *Ich bin ja noch ein Kind* the poet also laments the fact that he does not know and share the fate of animals and things, cats, horses, lamps, hats, and even the wind. Hereby he makes it clear that in his work he deals with the question of individuation in an absolute sense, far beyond the effect of a specific social organization on the existence of certain groups of people, although in details the poem has pronounced social-critical aspects. "Nie war ich ein Kind, zermalmt in den Fabriken/Dieser elenden Zeit, mit Ärmchen, ganz benarbt!"

God is regarded in this poem as being present in all suffering things—the omnipresence for which the poet himself yearns.

> Du aber, Herr, stiegst nieder, auch zu mir.
> Und hast die tausendfache Qual gefunden,
> Du hast in jedem Weib entbunden,
> Und starbst im Kot, in jedem Stück Papier,
> In jedem Zirkusseehund wurdest Du geschunden,
> Und Hure warst Du manchem Kavalier!

The poet beseeches this omnipresent God to grant him the same universality in the repeated exclamation "O Herr, zerreisse mich!" When he, too, dies in every "Lumpen," "Katze," "Gaul," and "Soldat," and is dispersed in the wind, existing in all things, even in smoke, then the words "Wir sind," which so far he has used intuitively, will really become a concrete and meaningful expression of the unity of all Creation.

Ich bin ja noch ein Kind is but one of several poems in which Werfel manifests this attitude and calls upon God to end his painful isolation from the rest of the world. Very typical in this respect is his adaptation of the traditional Pentecostal motif *Veni Creator Spiritus*, the first stanza of which concisely summarizes the despair at the fact of his individuation and the object of his profoundest desire.

> Komm, heiliger Geist, Du schöpferisch!
> Den Marmor unsrer Form zerbrich!

40

Dass nicht mehr Mauer krank und hart
Den Brunnen dieser Welt umstarrt,
Dass wir gemeinsam und nach oben
Wie Flammen ineinander toben!

The yearning for cosmic unification in God reaches a climax with the lines:

Dass alle wir in Küssens Überflüssen
Nur Deine reine heilige Lippe küssen!

This poem thus marks the extreme in the development of that type of expressionistic writing which has an almost desperate recourse to religious postulates in an endeavor to substantiate its faith in the basic, potential qualities of mankind.

The foregoing interpretations have, with the aid of specific texts, shown that expressionist writings fall into three broad categories, depending on the emphasis that is placed on the destruction of the old order, and, where applicable, the nature of the evoked ideal. Even the few examples considered demonstrate the wide variety of methods, determined by talent and genre, with which each of the three basic patterns can be realized. This diversity may make it difficult to recognize at first glance the relationship between works belonging to one group, as, for instance, Sternheim's *Die Hose* and Goll's *Der Panamakanal*. The decisive point is, however, that beyond such questions of specific execution, the writings concerned manifest the same attitude as regards the postulated ideal and the rejection of the status quo. It may be said that to be regarded as part of the body of expressionist writing, a work should either *contain a violent attack on the existing order,* which is contrasted only by implication or in vague allusions with an unspecified ideal; *or take the destruction of the status quo more or less for granted to dwell on visions of a socio-political, or, alternately, of a humanistic-anarchic nature.*

In addition to displaying characteristics conforming to any of these three extreme types, or a possible intermediate position between them, *an expressionist work,* because of the writers' desire to gain concrete results with it, *is rhetorical.* In fact, most of the attempts to define a typical pattern of linguistic usage seem to be based mainly on the rhetorical elements in expressionism. There are, however, many often mutually contradictory ways in which a piece of writing can clamor for attention and attempt to influence the public, while, moreover, the rhetorical effect

41

often depends at least as much on the actual vocabulary used as on the linguistic and syntactic devices employed.

A survey of the works, which in the foregoing have been interpreted from another viewpoint, shows the multitude of rhetorical devices employed even in such a limited number of examples. In Gustav Sack's poem the most obvious of these devices are the exclamatory tone and the repetition of the first line; the "rhetorical" questions introducing the third stanza; unlyrical and crude expressions designed to shock the sense of propriety of the bourgeois, such as "Dreck," "verdreckt," "Unzuchtpfuhl," and a tendency towards colloquial, popular turns of phrase such as "Bude" and " 'ne" instead of "eine."

In Georg Heym's poem *Der Krieg* the will to reach and affect an audience is manifest mainly in the heavy monotony of the metre. Each line rolls on with the irresistible finality of fate itself; the verses mercilessly pound on the reader's or hearer's mind with terrifying force and regularity.

Both *Die Hose* by Carl Sternheim and Reinhard Sorge's *Der Bettler*, as plays written to be performed before an audience, show that they seek an effect and a resonance by the very fact that they are dramas. The rhetorical tendency inherent in the genre is further heightened, in the case of Sternheim, through the liberal use of irony and satire, and in Sorge's work through shockingly grotesque scenes such as that in which the father for lack of red ink pierces a bird with his compasses.

In Iwan Goll's *Der Panamakanal* the devices of enumeration and accumulation are in evidence, while the frequent repetition of such words as "alle," "jeder," "jenes" also plays a role in the present context. Typical for Werfel's poems *An den Leser, Ich bin ja noch ein Kind,* and *Veni Creator Spiritus* are the vocative and exclamatory tone of many verses, while in Ernst Wilhelm Lotz' *Aufbruch der Jugend* the rhetorical attitude is clear in the use of "wir," the violent vocabulary and the vehement rhythm.

As these few instances indicate, the many ways in which a rhetorical effect can be achieved make it quite impracticable to formulate a rule defining this aspect of expressionism.[28] Moreover, the rhetorical appeal to the audience is by no means restricted to expressionism—in a sense it is even inherent in certain literary genres such as the drama. The rhetorical quality of a work can therefore not be used as a criterion to determine whether a given work should be considered part of the expressionist movement. On the other hand, the *absence* of a rhetorical attitude in

28. See Introduction.

writing which otherwise does fit into one of the three expressionist patterns would indicate the work concerned does not spring from the fundamental expressionist experience of reluctant outsidership and consequent ambivalence towards society. Such a work should therefore not be assigned to the movement.

In practice, the question whether a certain piece of writing does or does not belong to expressionism itself will only occur in the case of temporally closely related or contemporaneous work. Of greater significance than such problems of "labeling" specific works is the matter of determining the expressionist influence on later literature—not in an ideological, but in a formal sense. Practically every treatise on present-day authors finds occasion to claim such connections between them and the expressionists.[29]

29. See, for instance, Duwe; Soergel and Hohoff; Fritz Martini, *Deutsche Literaturgeschichte von den Anfängen bis zur Gegenwart* (Stuttgart, 1948 and later).

4. THE PATTERN OF PATHOS

The definition of the three main types of expressionist writing is inadequate for evaluating how closely work of other periods may be stylistically related to expressionism. A criterion must be sought which is independent of such themes and topics as hatred of Wilhelmian Germany or faith in a communist paradise. The negativistic, socio-political, and anarchic-humanistic subdivisions in the body of expressionist writing do, to be sure, represent abstractions from the multifarious ways in which the authors gave literary expression to their emotions and opinions concerning the human condition. Nevertheless, the literary categories thus obtained are still largely determined by the substance of the texts concerned, and are therefore still closely linked to the authors' ideas and intentions.

Now the purely structural elements in the definitions of the three variants of expressionism must be abstracted from those involving the substance, and a common denominator found. In the foregoing, the knowledge that the expressionists' world view conformed to one of three types helped to reduce the almost unlimited diversity of expressionist writing to three basic patterns. Similarly the socio-psychological facts serve to illuminate the question of the collective stylistic formula which combines the essential structural features of the three variants of expressionism. The different attitudes of mind of the expressionists were variants of one fundamental, Nietzsche-influenced reaction to their outsidership. They wanted to overcome their isolation, at the same time redeeming mankind by destroying the old order and establishing a better mode of life. They might conceive the objects of their hatred and hope in individual, social, or cosmic terms, but no matter in what particular embodiment or shape the social realities and ideals were perceived by the individual, he always rejected something and longed for something else.

Couched in these purposely vague terms, the basic mental outlook can be used to reconstruct the basic expressionist stylistic principle which unifies the three corresponding kinds of writing. This purely structural common denominator of all literature traditionally and unambiguously classed as expressionist is thus revealed to lie in its antithetic character. This antithesis, moreover, is not static, but dynamic, in the sense that the tension between the poles must inevitably lead to the destruction of one, while the other becomes absolute. The structure of expressionist

44

writing thus indicates that the situation it deals with is not stable, but that a force is at work which will resolve the existing polarity. The given antithesis is, however, not going to disappear in a Hegelian synthesis of the opposing poles, but in the complete ascendancy of one pole over the other.

Apart from these characteristics, all expressionist literature, as has been pointed out, is further marked by a rhetorical attitude. Although the latter cannot be satisfactorily reduced to specific linguistic and stylistic usages, nevertheless it must in some way be evident in the structure of the works.

Herewith it becomes possible to identify three fundamental structural aspects, which together constitute a stylistic criterion of literary expressionism. *The expressionist style is antithetic, dynamic, and rhetorical.* For the purpose of placing expressionism in a wider perspective, it is of interest to determine whether the combination of the structural elements of antithesis, dynamism, and rhetoric can be translated into the traditional terminology of poetics. It seems opportune to approach this question by investigating the style of expressionism to see whether it corresponds to the stylistic concept of pathos. The word "pathos" played a very prominent part in the terminology of the expressionists themselves. Thus Rudolf Leonhard in 1916 published an essay *Vom Pathos;* Franz Werfel's first collection of poetry *Der Weltfreund* includes a poem entitled *An mein Pathos*; the Neue Club established in the year 1911 the Neopathetische Cabaret in which a new pathos was proclaimed; and in 1913 Paul Zech and others started publishing a periodical called *Das Neue Pathos,* for which Stefan Zweig wrote a declaration of editorial principles under the same title.

Subsequent commentators have also used this word without, however, defining it adequately. Still, its frequent occurrence in secondary sources does reveal a general, if imprecise, awareness of the movement's distinguishing stylistic traits. In this context Fritz Martini may be mentioned, for he explicitly ascribes an exalted pathos to all expressionistic writing.[1] Wolfgang Paulsen also writes about pathos and "eine Art neuer Pathetik" as characteristic elements of expressionist literature.[2] Wilhelmina Stuyver calls pathos the "Lebensgrundstimmung . . . der Ausdruckskünstler."[3] Of the individual authors, to give some examples,

1. *Was war Expressionismus?* p. 33.
2. *Expressionismus und Aktivismus. Eine typologische Untersuchung* (Bern, 1935).
3. *Die deutsche expressionistische Dichtung im Lichte der Philosophie der Gegenwart* (Amsterdam, 1939), p. 133.

45

such dissimilar figures as Becher, Rubiner, Hasenclever, Heym, and Werfel are credited with pathos.[4]

In order to determine whether this frequently used term is really applicable to the common, unifying stylistic qualities of the writings usually classified as expressionistic, it is necessary—against the custom which has hitherto prevailed in secondary works on this subject—to define its meaning objectively.

In the history of German literature the word "pathos" occurs in several contexts. It may refer to the moral-ethical substance of a work. This is the view represented by Schiller, who stressed that pathos illuminates the spiritual freedom of mankind by demonstrating the superiority of reason (Vernunft) over nature. Man must, through his intellect, conquer the sorrows to which as a sentient creature he is subjected. The essence of Schillerian pathos is that the will successfully resists the emotions. "Das *Sinnenwesen* muss tief und heftig *leiden*; Pathos muss da sein, damit das Vernunftwesen seine Unabhängigkeit kundtun und sich handelnd darstellen könne."[5]

It is clear that for most expressionists pathos in this sense does not play any role. In Heym's case, for instance, there is no question of humanity having any spiritual freedom: it is absolutely subjected to nature, and must defenselessly suffer everything fate inflicts on it. In the world of Heym's writings, man invariably suffers, but, lacking all will power or intellect, he has to endure passively, thereby manifesting his utter helplessness in the face of forces beyond his control.

This amounts to a complete reversal of Schiller's ideas. No other expressionist appears to conform to them either. In no case is there any suggestion that mankind could overcome its sufferings by voluntarily accepting them. The cause of its sorrow—usually specified as the social organization—has to be removed or eliminated before happiness can be found.

If pathos in Schiller's moral-ethical sense is thus irreconcilable with the expressionists' outlook on life, this may be at least partly due to their reaction to one specific aspect of their upbringing. It has been pointed out that the older generations exploited the educational process as a means of defending the status quo against the rebellious tendencies of their children. Since these conservative tendencies were not justifiable

---

4. See, respectively, Friedmann and Mann, pp. 183, 67, 96; Fritz Martini, *Deutsche Literaturgeschichte*, p. 515; Friedmann and Mann, p. 96.

5. Schiller, "Über das Pathetische," *Sämtliche Werke*, V (München, 1959), 512.

from any rational viewpoint, they were reinforced by hollow idealism. Besides the classical authors of antiquity, Schiller was most intensively misused to distort the world image of youth in the interest of the Establishment. The result was that these adolescents, insofar as they were aware of the falsity of the officially propounded views, grew up with a profound mistrust of everything idealistic. This skepticism extended, of course, to the typically idealistic concept of moral freedom and its main embodiment in the writings of Friedrich Schiller.[6]

In this way the inflation of spurious idealism in the education and the public moral codex of Wilhelmian Germany tended to devaluate also the worthwhile aspects of this attitude of mind. The younger intellectuals, from whom the expressionists were recruited, had therewith inevitably become impervious to the idealistic side of the moral-ethical pathos concept. It is symptomatic that Kurt Hiller in the opening address of the Neopathetische Cabaret attacked the "geschmähte Schillerische" pathos.[7]

There is, however, a different side to pathos, which in Schiller's theoretical writing on the subject fails to receive its due attention. Schiller's bias towards the moral-ethical facet of pathos was a consequence of his philosophical position. As a Kantian thinker—his differences with the Königsberg philosopher are not relevant in the present context—his central idea was the autonomy of the human mind. It was this preoccupation which inevitably caused him to interpret pathos in terms of mankind's capacity for overcoming the suffering imposed by nature through a morally positive, voluntary acceptance of it. The framework in which man's freedom as a rational being manifested itself was the existing discrepancy between reality and ideal, the static presentation of which thus formed an essential part of pathos in Schiller's sense.

His views in this respect are most clearly expressed when he classifies pathos as a variant of satire, and defines the latter as the style which has for a subject the representation of the disparity of actuality and ideal.[8] Though this approach was entirely consistent with Schiller's philosophical tenets, it seems to be somewhat too narrow to do full justice to the

6. Cf. Friedrich Kummer, *Deutsche Literaturgeschichte des 19. und 20. Jahrhunderts,* 17-20th eds. (Dresden, 1924), I, 61: "Nicht zum wenigsten hat auch jahrzehntelang die deutsche Schule mit ihren entsetzlichen Erklärungen und Zergliederungen Schillerscher Balladen und Dramen die Jugend zum Widerspruch förmlich gezwungen."
7. *Die Weisheit der Langenweile,* Vol. I, p. 238.
8. Cf. Ernst Elster, *Prinzipien der Literaturwissenschaft,* Vol. II: *Stilistik* (Halle a/S, 1911), p. 48.

47

historically evolved meaning of the term "pathos." Ernst Elster therefore disagrees with Schiller and makes the point that in pathos the creative mind is not directed towards the incompatibility of reality and ideal, but towards the idea itself, in whose future realization or approximation the writer believes.[9]

Emil Staiger represents a similar view, which in his formulation reveals itself to be much less concerned with the substance of the literature concerned than Schiller's pathos-concept. "Es ist eine unmittelbare Bewegung, die sich selbst in ihrer Herkunft und Richtung nicht zu verstehen braucht. Im Unterschied zur lyrischen Bewegung aber hat sie beides, eine Herkunft und ein Ziel."[10] The definition of this style as a "direct movement" between two unspecified poles refers to the identical structural characteristics which in the foregoing pages, with reference to expressionism, were designated as antithesis and dynamism.

The "pathetic" artist has to convey his own dynamic impulse to his public, if ever the antithesis is to be resolved—and those whose resistance cannot be turned into cooperation through rhetorical persuasion must be destroyed so as not to endanger progress. This is also recognized by Staiger: "Der Dichter tut [dem Publikum] Gewalt an; und er will ihm Gewalt antun. Damit ist bereits gesagt, dass die pathetische Rede, abermals im Gegensatz zur lyrischen Sprache, ein Gegenüber voraussetzt, ein Gegenüber aber, das sie nicht, wie die epische, anerkennt, sondern aufzuheben trachtet, sei es so, dass der Redner den Hörer gewinnt, oder so, dass der Hörer von der Gewalt der Rede vernichtet wird."[11]

Thus Emil Staiger's remarks confirm that pathos in the traditional sense is defined by the same three qualities of antithesis, dynamism, and rhetoric that were found in the preceding pages to constitute the common denominator of expressionist style. In other words, *the stylistic criterion of expressionism can be designated as pathos.*

With this conclusion, the aim of defining the structural pattern of expressionist literature in terms derived from the theory of poetics has been achieved.

The complexity of the expressionist movement and the diversity of its literary manifestations prohibited the formulation of a definition which fixes technical or stylistic details. To find a unifying element of style it was necessary to resort to abstraction and generalization of the literary

---

9. Elster, pp. 48, 51.
10. *Grundbegriffe der Poetik,* 2nd ed. (Zürich, 1951), p. 155.
11. *Ibid.,* p. 153.

data. The lowest common denominator of the non-substantial characteristics of expressionist writing was found to pertain to the level of general structural patterns. Thus the criterion of expressionist style inevitably lacks more specific factors than those contained in the notions of antithesis, dynamism, and rhetoric, in the meaning of these terms developed in the preceding pages. This circumstance naturally affects the precision and exclusiveness of the definition which may, and does in fact, also apply to certain other works. The practical usefulness is not, however, affected by this, because it does not fit the literature of any period close enough in time to the expressionist era to cause any confusion. It may in this context be reiterated that the present study approaches the problem under discussion from a practical viewpoint. The stylistic definition of expressionism now arrived at is not intended to be "der Weisheit letzter Schluss" or a substitute for common sense. No matter how perfectly it may apply to a certain text, a work written by Goethe or one dating from the seventeenth century should not be regarded as expressionist.

But the broadness of the definition does not only leave its pragmatic value unimpaired; the broadness is actually an advantage. The reduction of expressionism to a general structural pattern, described in terms flexible enough to be applicable to works of other centuries dealing with different topics, opens up a historical perspective. The definition which, because of its abstract character, could be interpreted in terms of traditional poetic theory, therewith not only yields a convenient summarizing "label," but also illuminates certain aspects of the relationship between expressionism and the German literary heritage. It can serve, for instance, to reduce to correct proportions the affiliation between expressionism and baroque, which has been over-emphasized by such commentators as Ferdinand Josef Schneider and Wolfgang Paulsen. The latter in particular continually equates the two movements and calls expressionism an "Aufleben der Barockkunst des 17. Jahrhunderts."[12]

On the basis of the foregoing findings concerning the substance and structure of expressionism, both it and the baroque can be classified as temporally defined realizations of the abstract stylistic conception of pathos. What is denoted by the term "baroque" is the unique form, determined by a unique complex of political, sociological, psychological, and literary-historical factors, in which pathos was embodied during the seventeenth century. The baroque employs pathos to deal with the relationship between man and God. Expressionism, on the other hand, is

---

12. Schneider, *Der expressive Mensch*, pp. 59-60; Paulsen, *Expressionismus und Aktivismus*, p. 132.

a realization of the stylistic principle of pathos which, shaped by the conditions prevailing in Wilhelmian Germany, is concerned primarily with the relations between man and man.

The recognition of traditional pathos as the stylistic substratum of expressionist writing also throws some light on certain developments and differences within the movement. Since pathos aims at affecting the audience, it is a point of some interest in what way and through which human faculties this is to be achieved. In traditional pathos the answer to this question is quite clear: the audience is to be swayed or shattered *via* its emotional susceptibility. This appears from Willi Flemming's interpretation of a remark by Martin Opitz on the highly "pathetic" baroque tragedy. "Der barocke Tragiker will sein Publikum aufwühlen und überwältigen. Bezeichnend schreibt Opitz in der Trostschrift: 'Ein grosses Betrübnis lässt sich von sanften Worten nicht abweisen: Es will mit *Kräfften* überwunden seyn / und ist wie eine Nessel // welche, wann man sie stark angreifft nachgiebt / hergegen wann man gelinde mit ihr umbgeht zu brennen pflegt.' Wegen dieser seiner Kunsttendenz zielt der Dramatiker nicht auf die kühlen Bezirke des Hirns, sondern auf die warmen Ströme des Gefühles, ja der Leidenschaft, kurz: sein Drama ruht auf der Schicht des Emotionalen."[13]

Flemming's opinion that the effect of pathos was the excitation of the passions and emotions rather than the stimulation of the intellect is confirmed by other commentators. Emil Staiger defines pathos as a mode of expression which "die Leidenschaften erregt."[14] Heinrich Wölfflin declares that the baroque "will packen mit der Gewalt des Affekts, unmittelbar, überwältigend. Was er gibt, ist nicht gleichmässige Belebung, sondern Aufregung, Ekstase, Berauschung."[15] Among the seventeenth century authorities on poetics the same insight into the nature of the baroque style prevailed; Augustus Buchner saw it as the task of the poet to induce in the reader a "beständige Bewegung durch Bewunderung."[16]

Whereas rhetorical pathos in the traditional sense thus aims at affecting the public by stirring its passions, the expressionist movement in some of its manifestations deviated slightly from the tradition in this particular aspect of "pathetic" style. Expressionism underwent a development

---

13. Flemming, *Barockdrama, Deutsche Literatur in Entwicklungsreihen, Reihe Barock,* Vol. I (Leipzig, 1930), p. 16.
14. *Grundbegriffe der Poetik,* p. 151.
15. Quoted in Friedmann and Mann, p. 21.
16. Quoted in De Boor and Newald, *Geschichte der deutschen Literatur,* V (München, 1951), 21.

whose early phases are represented by the views on this subject prevailing in the Neue Club. These were expounded by Erwin Loewenson, on the occasion of the first performance of the Neopathetische Cabaret, in a manifesto which has remained unpublished; however, its substance can be deduced from later essays by its author.[17]

According to Loewenson, mankind should recognize the integral essence of the world behind the apparent chaos. This mystic aim could only be achieved if all spiritual forces were engaged harmoniously in the process of living. The decisive part in the propagation of this doctrine was assigned to the writers who, consciously or unconsciously, should express it in their works. Loewenson's ideas, which represented those of the majority of the Neue Club members, had been substantially influenced by the impression which the personality and physical appearance of Georg Heym had made on them. Even before Heym joined their society, around New Year, 1910, they had subscribed to a vitalistic-metaphysical conception of life and art. The intuitive force which they claimed to discern in Heym's personality as well as in his work seemed to confirm their ideas, and in this way caused them to attempt to expand their thoughts into a comprehensive philosophical system.

The president of the club, Kurt Hiller, and a few others had too cerebral an attitude to be able to endorse these views, and this difference of opinion contributed to the schism in the Neue Club in the spring of 1911. Yet Hiller was in substantial agreement with Erwin Loewenson about the point which in the present context is the most vital one. For him, too, pathos concerned the entire personality or the totality of the mental faculties. He succinctly defined it as "erhöhte psychische Temperatur."[18]

This deviation in the Neue Club from the orthodox conception of pathos as an excitement of the passions only, was probably connected with the influence of the French symbolists. It is significant that Heym greatly admired Baudelaire, whom he felt akin to and whom he ranked first among his literary gods.[19] It is particularly important to note that Baudelaire absorbed the poetic theories of Edgar Allan Poe and partly translated his essays into French. In this way the American's theses be-

---

17. "Bemerkungen über das 'Neopathos'" in Georg Heym, *Gesammelte Gedichte,* ed. Carl Seelig, pp. 243 ff; "Jakob van Hoddis. Erinnerungen mit Lebensdaten," in Jakob van Hoddis, *Weltende. Gesammelte Gedichte,* ed. Paul Pörtner (Zürich, 1958), pp. 96 ff; *Georg Heym oder vom Geist des Schicksals* (Hamburg, München, 1962).

18. *Die Weisheit der Langenweile,* I, 237.

19. See his diary entry of 11.5.1910.

came known in Germany.[20] Poe maintained that the effect of a poem should be an "intensive and pure elevation of the soul and not of intellect or heart." The satisfaction of the rational faculties and the appeal to the heart could, of course, also be introduced in a poem, but only in "proper subservience to the predominant aim" of elevating the soul.[21] Poe's theory remains somewhat obscure because it is not entirely clear what he meant by an elevation of the soul. Hugo Friedrich interprets it as "eine umfassende Gestimmtheit."[22] This interpretation accentuates the similarity between the ideas of Poe which were transmitted by Baudelaire and the attitude exemplified by Loewenson's philosophy.

Apart from him and his fellow members of the early and short-lived Neue Club, however, the expressionists, in agreement with the orthodox "pathetic" attitude on this point, chose to concentrate on stirring the passions of their public. This approach was explicitly represented by the periodical *Das Neue Pathos* which Paul Zech founded in 1913. In the second issue Stefan Zweig published a salient essay which left no doubt about the orthodoxy of the pathos promoted by this journal. "Wieder wie einst scheint heute der lyrische Dichter befähigt, wenn nicht der geistige Führer der Zeit, so doch der Bändiger und Erreger ihrer Leidenschaften zu werden, der Rhapsode, der Anrufende, Befeuernde, der Entfachende des heiligen Feuers: der Energie."[23] Rudolf Leonhard expressed a similar traditional conception of pathos when he concisely defined it as the "leidenschaftliche Bewusstheit eines Zustands."[24]

20. See Otto Pick's article on the German translation of Baudelaire's works, in *Die Aktion,* May 1, 1912.

21. Poe, "The Philosophy of Composition," in *The Complete Works,* (New York, 1902), I, 292-93.

22. *Die Struktur der modernen Lyrik* (Hamburg, 1956), p. 26.

23. Quoted on p. 47 of Catalogue No. 7 *Expressionismus. Literatur und Kunst 1910-1923* of the Schiller-Nationalmuseum, Marbach a.N.

24. *Vom Pathos. Aus Aeonen des Fegefeuers* (Berlin, 1916), quoted by Paul Pörtner, *Literaturrevolution 1910-1925. Dokumente. Manifeste. Programme.* Vol. I: *Zur Aesthetik und Poetik,* Vol. XIII in "die mainzer reihe" (Neuwied, 1960), p. 143.

5. THE DEFINITION AT WORK

The conclusion that pathos is the hallmark of expressionist style has in the foregoing pages proved useful in clarifying certain variations within the expressionist movement as well as its literary-historical connections. However, the primary aim of the present study was to find a practical yardstick of expressionism, a criterion by which specific texts can be gauged objectively and uniformly on their possible expressionist elements.

In the course of the inquiry it has been found expedient to distinguish between the characteristic qualities of work actually representing the movement, and those of writings exhibiting a purely formal, structural affinity with expressionism. In the former, the substance with which the expressionists filled the "pathetic" stylistic mold of their works is of supreme importance. The particular realization of pathos which is known as expressionism is distinguished from other literature in the same style by virtue of the fact that the antithesis is between the old social order and a new, ideal human world. To be attributable to the movement, a text has to be rhetorical, and reveal the negativistic or the socio-political or the humanistic-anarchic variant of this fundamental dynamic antithesis. There may, of course, emerge, at any time in history, writers who deal with this subject matter in this style. Only during the period from about 1910 to 1920, however, did such writing completely dominate the literary scene and assume the collective character of a movement. The application of common sense and literary taste usually suffices to decide whether authors of other periods whose work is expressionist both in substance and structure are temporally isolated kindred souls or imitators.

When it is not a matter of assigning specific texts to the expressionist movement, but of tracing purely stylistic affinities, the substance of expressionist pathos is not to be taken into consideration. In these cases only the structural elements are decisive. Since the structure of expressionist writing corresponds to the "pathetic" pattern of style, it is obvious that stylistic similarity with expressionism links a work to all "pathetic" literature. If the aim is to place the text concerned stylistically in a literary-historical context, this expansion of the frame of reference has the same advantages that were apparent in dealing with expressionism as a whole. In case possible expressionist influence on later literature has to be established, the wider applicability of the term "pathos" does not impair its usefulness either. It seems a reasonably safe assumption that a young twentieth century writer is more likely to undergo a strong impact from, say, Georg Heym's work, than from that of Heinrich Anshelm von Ziegler und Kliphausen. If thus the conclusions reached concerning expressionist literature and style are not disqualified because of their lack of exclusiveness, their usefulness still remains to be tested with concrete examples. The position of some works which are recognized to be on the borderline of the expressionist movement will therefore in the following pages be clarified with the aid of the three basic types of writing found within it.

These may first be used to illuminate the case of Georg Trakl, who is traditionally classified as one of the leading early expressionists, and yet is often felt to be quite different from the others. Commentators frequently reveal this ambiguity by pointing to specific aspects in which Trakl stands apart from the usual expressionist pattern. Thus, Ferdinand Josef Schneider makes the observation, "Trakl allein weiss unter den modernen Lyrikern, dass sich Armut, Not und verkümmertes Menschentum auch auf dem Lande findet. . . ."[1] Kasimir Edschmid points out that Trakl's "Gemüt melancholischer und sein Vers inniger und die heimliche Musik seines Gedichts durch ihre leisen Schwingungen tönender ist" than is usual in expressionism. However, he disagrees with those who for this reason exclude Trakl from this movement.[2] Alfred Richard Meyer calls Trakl an "Elegiker, der sich schon in Kurt Wolffs *Jüngstem Tag* neben Ferdinand Hardekopf, Walter Hasenclever, Emmy Hennings, Ludwig Rubiner, Ernst Wilhelm Lotz, Paul Kraft, Otfried Krzyzanowski, Paul Boldt, Arthur Drey als Hofmannsthal-Klassizist und zugleich als verdunkelte Hölderlin-Parallele etwas absonderlich ausnahm."[3]

Trakl's biography shows that he underwent the expressionists' usual forlornness and loneliness, while in his case the feeling of being an outsider was further stimulated by his position as a Protestant in a Roman Catholic environment. Walter Sokel describes how his family's lack of understanding drove Trakl deeper and deeper into isolation.[4] Fritz Martini writes, "Er hasste den Zeitgeist, der sich dem Wahn der Macht, des Erfolges, des Goldes taumelnd verschrieb und sich dem Göttlichen

1. *Der expressive Mensch,* pp. 145-46.
2. *Lebendiger Expressionismus. Auseinandersetzungen. Gestalten. Erinnerungen* (Basel, 1961), pp. 246-47.
3. *die maer von der musa expressionistica* (Düsseldorf, 1948). pp. 60-61.
4. *The Writer in Extremis,* pp. 72-73.

54

verweigerte, den Dichter aber in das Heimatlose verstiess—heimatlos in der Zeit, heimatlos aber auch vor Gott, als dessen verlorener Sohn Trakl sich fühlte."[5]

Trakl reacted to his loneliness, not by endeavoring to establish contact with his fellow men, but by withdrawing completely within himself. It is significant that the extreme inversion which marked his private behavior also characterizes his poetry; the motivation and effect of his works coincide. Martini writes in this context, "Er erfuhr, dass die Seele im Irdisch-Wirklichen fremd und heimatlos geworden sei, sie allein aber galt. Nur indem er immer tiefer in sich hinein, in sie hinunterstieg, vermochte er in ihre Stille einzukehren. Trakl war ganz und nur er selbst, wesenhaft in sich beschlossen, daher kennzeichnet alle seine Verse die Stille und Monotonie des Monologs, das Eintönige und Raunende, das mehr verschweigt als ausspricht."[6]

Because it only refers to his own soul, Trakl's poetry represents the radical opposite of the attitude of expressionism, which looked beyond the poet's own personality at society. The soliloquy is also irreconcilable with rhetoric which is directed at, and for its existence depends on, a public. The relationship between Trakl and the expressionists is thus limited to their common sociological situation. Trakl's reaction to his outsidership made him turn away altogether from the problems of human society with which the typical expressionists continued to occupy themselves in their work. To Trakl social reality in all its aspects was only significant insofar as it affected or symbolized his own private emotions, whereas to the typical expressionists the social reality, including the man-to-man relationship among people of all classes, was all-important in its own right. If the term expressionism is used to designate a purely sociological aspect of literature, referring to those writings which are motivated by a specific type of relationship existing between author and society, then Trakl is certainly an expressionist. If, however, our yardstick of expressionist writing is applied, Trakl is definitely not an expressionist, because his work is unrhetorical and not primarily concerned with the antithesis of social reality and ideal.

Another figure on the fringe of the movement is Alfred Mombert, who is chronologically on the early border of the period. In his works he displays an absolutely egocentric attitude in such lines as: "Da Ich. Ich finde mich auf einem Thron"; "Ich stehe gekettet auf schwarzer Fläche; /gesunken in Mich"; "Ich bin die Heimat." This preoccupation with the self may amount to self-deification: "Meine Hände legen sich gött-

---

5. *Was war Expressionismus?* p. 114.　　　6. *Ibid.,* p. 115.

lich auf die Flammen."[7] Humanity and nature are only perceived as a background to the person of the poet. In this poetic universe there is no trace of the consciousness of social realities which underlies expressionism, nor the urge either to "destroy" the reader or to persuade him of the validity of the writer's conceptions.

Another dubious case is Else Lasker-Schüler, who is customarily associated with expressionism. She is primarily interested in the individual relationship between herself and another person, or between herself and God. In her case, as in that of Mombert, humanity as such and for its own sake does not play a role. Her poetry is primarily a lament about her own unhappiness, but it does not place her fate in the larger context of the human situation. "Sie allein ist Inhalt ihrer Dichtungen."[8] Her work has primarily the character of a soliloquy, and does not aim at affecting the public as expressionism does. Neither Mombert nor Else Lasker-Schüler should therefore be regarded as expressionists.

Another poet usually classified as a precursor or early exponent of expressionism, Theodor Däubler does justify this classification. His very extensive production includes purely impressionistic works, but for the present purpose it is decisive that even before 1910 he included in his *Nordlicht* lines such as the following:

Der Mensch muss fliegen! der Mensch muss fliegen! verbreitet den
                Sturm!
Vertilgt im Herzen, vertilgt im Leibe den furchtsamen Wurm!
Ersehnt im Winde, erhofft im Winde den wehenden Geist!
Beruft im Dunkel das Kind der Sterne, das Schweben verheisst!
Erträumt Gefahren, erfiebert Schrecken, entfesselt das leid!
Kometen helfen. Gestirne drohen. Erfasst euch im Streit!
Den Wurm ertötet, den Wurm verachtet, verwundet den Wurm.[9]

In the manner typical of expressionism Däubler here violently opposes the "Wurm" of the spirit of his age, which in many other poems he attacks by means of ironical descriptions of bourgeois life.

Seht, wie die Finger flink ihr Geld zusammenscharren!
Stets achtsam hat man die Havannas ausgeschachtelt,
Fakturen quadratiert und durch sich selbst geachtelt.[10]

7. Respectively, *Ein Anhauch kam . . . ; Die Tat; Die Terrasse; Die Terrasse;* all in *Lyrik des expressionistischen Jahrzehnts.*
8. Albert Soergel, *Dichtung und Dichter der Zeit. Neue Folge. Im Banne des Expressionismus* (Leipzig, 1925), p. 440.
9. "Das Sternenkind," *Dichtungen und Schriften* (München, 1956), p. 860.
10. "Hesperien III," in *Dichtungen und Schriften,* p. 153.

Against the pedestrian materialism of his time, he asserted his yearning for excitement and more intense emotions, and the supremacy of the spirit. His confidence in the justness of his cause appears from the conviction that cosmic forces will help in the struggle. The exclamatory style and the consistent use of the imperative show these lines to be emphatically directed at a public which they were to sway in accordance with the poet's views. The passages quoted thus conform in every respect to that type of expressionism which concentrates on the attack on the old order, and conveys only a vague, unspecific vision of the ideal which is to replace it. Consequently Däubler, at least in part of his work, must be considered an early exponent of the expressionist movement.

Finally, a concrete example may demonstrate how the possible affinity of later writers with expressionism can be investigated by determining if the structure of their work, in conformity with the stylistic pattern of pathos, is antithetic, dynamic, and rhetorical. A suitable object for this purpose can be found among the works of the present-day lyricist and radio-play author Günter Eich. Both the chronological facts—he was born in 1907—and the general atmosphere of his writing make it perfectly obvious that Eich is not an expressionist. Yet there is something reminiscent of expressionism in his work. Fritz Martini acknowledges this when he writes about him, "Es zeichnet sich ein Darstellungsstil ab, der von der Lyrik des Expressionismus nach dem ersten Weltkrieg weit entfernt und gleichwohl durch sie hindurchgegangen ist. . . ."[11]

An examination of Eich's poem *Ende eines Sommers* which opens his poetry collection *Botschaften des Rengens*,[12] may illuminate the points of contact and the differences with expressionism.

Wer möchte leben ohne den Trost der Bäume!

Wie gut, dass sie am Sterben teilhaben!
Die Pfirsiche sind geerntet, die Pflaumen färben sich,
während unter dem Brückenbogen die Zeit rauscht.

Dem Vogelzug vertraue ich meine Verzweiflung an.
Er misst sein Teil von Ewigkeit gelassen ab.
Seine Strecken
werden sichtbar im Blattwerk als dunkler Zwang,
die Bewegung der Flügel färbt die Früchte.

Es heisst Geduld haben.
Bald wird die Vogelschrift entsiegelt,
unter der Zunge ist der Pfennig zu schmecken.

11. *Deutsche Literaturgeschichte*, p. 596.   12. Frankfurt/M, 1955.

It is obvious that in substance this poem is very different from the works of the expressionist movement. Eich does not allude once, be it openly or in metaphor, to an existing social order, nor to any kind of ideal world for which he yearns. On the other hand, the rhetorical attitude characteristic of expressionism is shared by *Ende eines Sommers*. The rhetorical question with which the poem begins, the exclamatory nature of the next line, and the adjuratory tone of the concluding three verses are evidence that the work aims at affecting an audience. This is not surprising, since this author's favorite medium is the "Hörspiel" which, like the stage play, depends as a genre on a confrontation with the public.

The structure of *Ende eines Sommers* is clearly antithetic, in that it is characterized by the two antipodal concepts of the finite and the infinite. The former is introduced in the direct reference to time and in the allusions to temporality contained in the notions of living, ripening, dying and harvesting. Infinity is mentioned directly—in the exact middle of the poem—and also obliquely in the obolus motif of the last verse which refers to the state of death. From Eich's general metaphoric usage it appears that the words "Vogelzug" and "Vogelschrift" must also be mentioned in this context, because the birds are among his most favored symbols of infinity. Thus the raven-like protagonist of his radio-play *Sabeth* turns out to be a representative of eternity. The usage of the bird-motif in such poems as *Der Grosse Lübbe-See, Tage mit Hähern, Mittags um zwei, Geisenhausen, In anderen Sprachen* and others confirms the connection between it and the realm of the Absolute.[13]

In *Ende eines Sommers* the polarity of the finite and infinity is not presented statically, but as an antithesis which an incontrovertible "dark force" will resolve. In death mankind is freed from the shackles of the finite and rejoins the realm of eternity from which his human individuality had excluded him. This inevitable death is, moreover, not merely recognized and acknowledged, but impatiently looked forward to. If the trees did not, by dying, reassure man that he, too, will soon overcome the limitations of his finite existence and be able to understand the essence of eternity, symbolized in the birds, life would be unbearable.

The dynamic ascendancy of one of the antithetic concepts over the other is thus, in this poem, very marked. Since the poem is structurally antithetic, dynamic, and rhetorical, it conforms to the pattern of pathos, and has a fundamental stylistic affinity with expressionist literature. The

---

13. See my article "Günter Eich and the Birds," *The German Quarterly*, Vol. XXXVII, No. 3, May, 1964.

question whether this relationship is to some extent due to direct influence can only be decided on the basis of biographical data. Even if, in this particular case, it should be so, then the expressionist example would only have stimulated the development of the inherent qualities of Eich's work. This work directly represents the archetypal realization of pathos, namely the rhetorical expression of man's despair at the fact of his individuation and his yearning to become one again with the mystical entity of the universe.

In expressionist literature, the basic antithesis is that of the existing world, in which man is totally isolated from his brethren, and a new, ideal order in which all humanity is one. In the perspective afforded by the definition of expressionism as pathos, however, this difference between expressionism and Eich's work, resolves itself on a higher level. Ultimately, the sociological preoccupation of expressionism is no more, and no less, than a symbolization of humanity's position in the face of eternity.

BOOK LIST

The following are the main works dealing with the expressionist movement as a whole.

Bruggen, M. F. E. van. *Im Schatten des Nihilismus. Die expressionistische Lyrik im Rahmen und als Ausdruck der geistigen Situation Deutschlands.* Amsterdam, 1946.

Duwe, Willi. *Deutsche Dichtung des 20. Jahrhunderts. Die Geschichte der Ausdruckskunst.* Zürich, Leipzig, 1936. New edition in 2 vols., Zürich, 1962.

Edschmid, Kasimir. *Lebendiger Expressionismus. Auseinandersetzungen. Gestalten. Erinnerungen.* Basel, 1961.

Expressionismus. Gestalten einer literarischen Bewegung, ed. Hermann Friedmann and Otto Mann. Heidelberg, 1956.

Expressionismus. Literatur und Kunst 1910-1923. Eine Ausstellung des Deutschen Literaturarchivs im Schiller-Nationalmuseum Marbach a.N. vom 8. Mai bis 31. Oktober 1960. (Sonderausstellungen des Schiller-Nationalmuseums Katalog Nr. 7), ed. Bernhard Zeller.

Martini, Fritz. *Was war Expressionismus?* Urach, 1948.

Meyer, Alfred Richard. *die maer von der musa expressionistica.* Düsseldorf, 1948.

Muschg, Walter. *Von Trakl zu Brecht.* München, 1961.

Paulsen, Wolfgang. *Expressionismus und Aktivismus. Eine typologische Untersuchung.* Bern, 1935.

Schneider, Ferdinand Josef. *Der expressive Mensch und die deutsche Lyrik der Gegenwart.* Stuttgart, 1927.

Soergel, Albert. *Dichtung und Dichter der Zeit. Neue Folge. Im Banne des Expressionismus.* Leipzig, 1925. New edition by Curt Hohoff, Düsseldorf, 1963.

Sokel, Walter H. *The Writer in Extremis. Expressionism in 20th Century German Literature.* Stanford, Calif., 1959. German translation under the title *Der literarische Expressionismus,* München, n.d.

Stuyver, Wilhelmina. *Die deutsche expressionistische Dichtung im Lichte der Philosophie der Gegenwart.* Amsterdam, 1939.

Thomas, R. Hinton, and Samuel, Richard. *Expressionism in German Life, Literature and the Theatre (1910-1924).* Cambridge, 1939.

See also the following research reports.

Martini, Fritz. "Deutsche Literatur zwischen 1880 und 1950. Ein Forschungsbericht," in *Deutsche Vierteljahrsschrift für Literaturwissenschaft und Geistesgeschichte,* XXVI (1952), 478-535. The section on expressionism: pp. 510-24.

Schneider, Karl Ludwig. "Neuere Literatur zur Dichtung des deutschen Expressionismus," in *Euphorion,* XLVII (1953), 99-110.

Konrad, Gustav. Untitled research report, in *Wirkendes Wort,* VII (1956-57), 351-65.

Brinkmann, Richard. *Expressionismus. Forschungs-Probleme 1952-1960.* Stuttgart, 1961. (Sonderdruck aus *Deutsche Vierteljahrsschrift für Literaturwissenschaft und Geistesgeschichte,* Vol. XXXIII, 1959, and Vol. XXXIV, 1960).

UNIVERSITY OF FLORIDA MONOGRAPHS

Humanities

No. 1 (Spring 1959): *The Uncollected Letters of
James Gates Percival.* Edited by Harry R. Warfel

No. 2 (Fall 1959): *Leigh Hunt's Autobiography
The Earliest Sketches.* Edited by Stephen F. Fogle

No. 3 (Winter 1960): *Pause Patterns in
Elizabethan and Jacobean Drama.* By Ants Oras

No. 4 (Spring 1960): *Rhetoric and American
Poetry of the Early National Period*
By Gordon E. Bigelow

No. 5 (Fall 1960): *The Background of*
The Princess Casamassima. By W. H. Tilley

No. 6 (Winter 1961): *Indian Sculpture in the
John and Mable Ringling Museum of Art*
By Roy C. Craven, Jr.

No. 7 (Spring 1961): *The Cestus. A Mask*
Edited by Thomas B. Stroup

No. 8 (Fall 1961): Tamburlaine, Part I
and Its Audience. By Frank B. Fieler

No. 9 (Winter 1962): *The Case of John Darrell
Minister and Exorcist.* By Corinne Holt Rickert

No. 10 (Spring 1962): *Reflections of the
Civil War in Southern Humor.* By Wade H. Hall

No. 11 (Fall 1962): *Charles Dodgson
Semeiotician.* By Daniel F. Kirk

No. 12 (Winter 1963): *Three Middle English
Religious Poems.* Edited by R. H. Bowers

No. 13 (Spring 1963): *The Existentialism
of Miguel de Unamuno.* By José Huertas-Jourda

No. 14 (Fall 1963): *Four Spiritual Crises
in Mid-Century American Fiction*
By Robert Detweiler

No. 15 (Winter 1964): *Style and Society
in German Literary Expressionism*
By Egbert Krispyn

UNIVERSITY OF FLORIDA PRESS / GAINESVILLE, FLORIDA